MATH PHONICS™

DECIMALS

Quick Tips and Alternative Techniques for Math Mastery

BY MARILYN B. HEIN
ILLUSTRATED BY RON WHEELER

Teaching & Learning Company

1204 Buchanan St., P.O. Box 10
Carthage, IL 62321-0010

THIS BOOK BELONGS TO

_____

ACKNOWLEDGEMENTS

Sincere thanks to my son, Adam, my brother, J.C. Vestring, to Nick and Jenny and my friend Karen Marvin for their suggestions and moral support. Also, thanks to my good friends Regina Cortner and Jed and Todd Shepherd.

DEDICATION

I would like to dedicate this book to my husband, Joe; our children, Gretchen, Troy, Adam, Sarah, Robert, Nick and Jenny; and my parents, Vincent and Cleora Vestring.

Cover by Ron Wheeler

Copyright © 1999, Teaching & Learning Company

ISBN No. 1-57310-200-8

Printing No. 987654321

Teaching & Learning Company
1204 Buchanan St., P.O. Box 10
Carthage, IL 62321-0010

Math Phonics™ is a trademark registered to Marilyn B. Hein.

TABLE OF CONTENTS

Dear Teacher or Parent,

Long division, fractions, decimals and percent!

Why do some people break out in a cold sweat at the thought of doing some of these problems? Why do so many adults freely admit that they hated math when they were in school?

Each person can probably find a different reason why math was difficult for him or her, but I believe most problems fall into one of these categories:

1. *The student did not understand the basic concept.*
2. *The student had difficulty in memorizing basic math facts and processes.*
3. *The student got bored before mastering all the important facts or processes.*
4. *The student had trouble following what the teacher was explaining in a class of 20 or 30.*

The Math Phonics™ series has specific materials for dealing with each of these problems. Basic concepts are explained and demonstrated by use of pages in each book—sometimes as a classroom demonstration conducted by the teacher and sometimes as a demonstration done by each student individually—sort of like chemistry lab. Once you do the experiment yourself, you are more likely to understand and remember it.

Each Math Phonics™ book has several memory "tricks" to help students remember important facts and processes. And to deal with boredom, books contain original games and drill activities and worksheets with a lot of variety.

Last of all, nearly every student needs a little one-on-one. There are several take-home materials and prepared notes for parents so they will know what they can do to help.

Teachers and parents have had great results using Math Phonics™ materials with students who needed extra help with math. Level 2 pages are included for those who catch on quickly and need more of a challenge. Three topics are included which give students a sense of power over numbers. They are Magic Squares, Figuring Tips and Guess Your Age. Everyone can learn them and they are fun.

Wouldn't it be wonderful to raise a generation of people who never said, "I hated math," but rather said, "I thought math was fun!" It's not impossible! Give it a try.

Sincerely,

Marilyn

Marilyn B. Hein

WHAT IS MATH PHONICS™?

Math Phonics™ is a specially designed program for introducing decimals or for remedial work.

WHY IS IT CALLED MATH PHONICS™?

In reading, phonics is used to group similar words, and it teaches the students simple rules for pronouncing each word.

In *Math Phonics™*, math concepts are learned by means of simple patterns, rules and wall charts with games for practice.

In reading, phonics develops mastery by repetitive use of words already learned.

Math Phonics™ uses drill and review to reinforce students' understanding. Manipulatives and practice games help reduce the "drill and kill" aspect.

HOW WAS MATH PHONICS™ DEVELOPED?

Why did "Johnny" have so much trouble learning to read during the years that phonics was dropped from the curriculum of many schools in this country? For the most part, he had to simply memorize every single word in order to learn to read, an overwhelming task for a young child. If he had an excellent memory or a knack for noticing patterns in words, he had an easier time of it. If he lacked those skills, learning to read was a nightmare, often ending in failure–failure to learn to read and failure in school.

Phonics seems to help many children learn to read more easily. Why? When a young child learns one phonics rule, that one rule unlocks the pronunciation of dozens or even hundreds of words. It also provides the key to parts of many larger words. The trend in U.S. schools today seems to be to include phonics in the curriculum because of the value of that particular system of learning.

Why do students seem to forget basic rules regarding decimals? (For example, keep decimals in a straight line for addition, count the decimal places after the decimals for multiplication.) I believe the main reason is that no one explained why these rules work–just taught them as shortcuts. This *Math Phonics™* book puts a lot of emphasis on **why** these rules work! The rules are then reinforced by wall charts, worksheets and games.

The name *Math Phonics™* occurred to me because the rules, patterns and memory techniques that I have assembled are similar to language arts phonics in several ways. Most of these rules are short and easy to learn. Children are taught to look for patterns and use them as "crutches" for coming up with the answer quickly. Some concepts have similarities so that learning one makes it easier to learn another. Last of all, *Math Phonics™* relies on lots of drill and review, just as language arts phonics does.

Children *must* master basic decimal concepts and the sooner the better. When I taught seventh and eighth grade math over 20 years ago, I was amazed at the number of students who had not mastered decimals. At that time, I had no idea how to help them. My college math classes did not give me any preparation for that situation. I had not yet delved into my personal memory bank to try to remember how I had mastered those basics.

When my own children had problems in that area, I was strongly motivated to give some serious thought to the topic. I knew my children had to master the basics, and I needed to come up with additional ways to help them. For kids to progress past the lower grades without a thorough knowledge of those concepts would be like trying to learn to read without knowing the alphabet.

I have always marveled at the large number of people who tell me that they "hated math" when they were kids. I firmly believe that a widespread use of *Math Phonics*™ could be a tremendous help in solving the problem of "math phobia."

WHAT ARE THE PRINCIPLES OF MATH PHONICS™?

There are three underlying principles of *Math Phonics*™.

They are: 1. Understanding
2. Learning
3. Mastery

Here is a brief explanation of the meaning of these principles.

1. **UNDERSTANDING:** All true mathematical concepts are abstract which means they can't be touched. They exist in the mind. For most of us, understanding such concepts is much easier if they can be related to something in the real world–something that can be touched.

   Thus, I encourage teachers to let students find answers for themselves by relating decimals to fractions. I think this helps the students to remember answers once they have discovered them on their own.

2. **LEARNING:** Here is where the rules and patterns mentioned earlier play an important part. A student can be taught a simple rule and on the basis of that, begin to practice with decimals. But the learning necessary for the basic decimal concepts must be firmly in place so that the information will be remembered next week, next month and several years from now. That brings us to the next principle.

3. **MASTERY:** We have all had the experience of memorizing some information for a test or quiz

tomorrow and then promptly forgetting most of it. This type of memorization will not work for decimals. In order for students to master decimals, *Math Phonics*™ provides visual illustrations, wall charts, manipulatives, worksheets and games. Some students may only need one or two of these materials, but there are plenty from which to choose for those who need more.

POCKET FOLDERS

You will want to purchase or create a pocket folder for each student to keep all the *Math Phonics*™ materials together.

Inexpensive pocket folders are available at many school or office supply stores, discount stores or other outlets.

An easy-to-make pocket folder can be made from a large paper grocery or shopping bag.

1. Cut away the bottom of the bag and discard.

2. Cut open along one long side and lay flat.

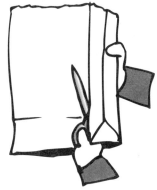

3. Pick one of the folds and measure out 10" (25 cm) from the fold on either side. Trim bag.

4. Now measure 12" (30 cm) down from the top and fold up the remaining portion of the bag.

5. Staple pockets at outside edges and fold in half.

6. Decorate front and back.

Suggest to parents that children should keep all of their *Math Phonics*™ materials (worksheets, fraction strips, wall charts, etc.) in this folder. Parents may also wish to supply clear plastic page protectors and dry-erase markers. Worksheets can be inserted into the page protectors, completed with the dry-erase marker and reused.

SUMMARY OF THE 10 BASIC STEPS

1. Understanding Decimals–Tenths

Review the meaning of a fraction. Show that a decimal is an easier way of writing fractions with a denominator of 10.

2. Hundredths

Show the second decimal place to write a fraction with a denominator of 100. Review the place value system.

3. Money

Show students how to think of money as a decimal. Have them think of coins as a fraction of a dollar. Introduce the idea of percent.

4. Addition and Subtraction of Decimals

Teach the technique of adding and subtracting with a decimal in the problem. Borrowing and carrying work regardless of where the decimal is placed. This step also includes **key words in problem solving** and a worksheet to practice finding key words. Starting with this step, an advanced worksheet–Level 2–is included with each set of pages.

5. Lining Up Decimals

Demonstrate why decimals must be kept in a straight line for addition and subtraction.

6. Multiplying Decimals

Demonstrate how to find the right answer using fractions or addition. Then teach the shortcut and why it works. The shortcut is to count the decimal places in the problem and place the same total number of decimal places in the answer.

7. Dividing Decimals

Show students how to find the right answer using fractions. Then show that the rules work and make the problem easier.

8. Ratios and Percents

Explain and demonstrate a ratio. Talk about percent and show how to change a fraction or a decimal to percent. Teach how to figure tips in a restaurant.

9. Fractions and Percents

Show how to change a proper fraction to decimal and percent. Teach shortcuts to finding percents of numbers.

10. Rules and Assessment

This step includes a summary page of rules and games. Also, assessment pages for Levels 1 and 2.

INTRODUCTION: Before discussing decimals, do a brief review of fractions.

Put the fraction 3/4 on the board. Ask students to explain what the two numbers mean.

Example: $\dfrac{3}{4}$ Numerator
            Denominator

A cake has been divided into four pieces. Three of the pieces have been eaten. Do the same with the fraction 5/6 and the fraction 9/10. Draw rectangles on the board to demonstrate 5/6 and 9/10.

The fraction 3/4 can also mean three out of four objects or people. If you have four people in your family and three have brown hair, you can say 3/4 of your family members have brown hair.

Note: If you have several students in your class who do not understand fractions, use the *Math Phonics™—Fractions* book to introduce or review fractions with them.

RULE: A fraction is a number that shows that something or a group of items has been divided. It has a numerator above the line and a denominator below the line.

DECIMALS: Whenever the denominator is 10, the fraction can be written with a decimal point. It is called a decimal fraction or decimal for short.

9/10 = .9

Both the fraction and the decimal are read as nine tenths.

For a whole number and a fraction with 10 as the denominator, you can also write it as a decimal.

2 9/10 = 2.9

Both are read two and nine tenths.

OPTIONAL: Give each student the activity page "Unit with Tenths" (page 12), a vinyl page protector, a facial tissue and a crayon. Students should insert the activity page into the protector. Ask each row of students to color in a fraction of the box. (2/10, 5/10, 7/10, etc.) Have them write it as a fraction and as a decimal.

FOLDERS: Each student should keep all handout materials and returned homework papers in a math folder.

HOMEWORK: Worksheets A and B are about equal in difficulty. You could do one in class, or skip B if all students are able to master A.

MATH HISTORY BONUS: The decimal point as we know it made its debut in 1617 in a book by Scotsman, John Napier. *

The Math History Bonus items can be presented to your students one at a time, lesson by lesson. Another use is to give each student a copy of page 11 which lists all of the Math History Bonus items together. They should keep these pages in their math notebooks or folders. For some of your students who grasp decimals easily and might become bored, you could let them work at their own speed and finish the decimal worksheets quickly and then choose one of these history facts as the basis for a research paper.

There is a lot more to math than just computation. Some people have a lot of trouble with computation, and we want to do all that we can to help them. For those who find it easy to compute the correct answer, we need to allow them some time to study how concepts were developed in the past so that they can develop new concepts in the future. If your school library does not have books on mathematicians and historical developments, try the internet.

*All Math History Bonus items are taken from *Mathematics*, Life Science Library, Time, Inc., New York.

MATH HISTORY BONUS ITEMS

1. The decimal point as we know it made its debut in 1617 in a book by Scotsman, John Napier.

2. The word *decimal* is based on the Latin word *decimus* meaning "tenth." The decimal system uses 10 numerals–0, 1, 2, 3, 4, 5, 6, 7, 8 and 9. This system was probably developed mainly because each human has 10 fingers.

3. A quarter is sometimes referred to as two *bits*. The word comes from a Spanish coin called a "real" or a "bit." Eight of them equalled a dollar.

   The first national leader to have his head stamped on a coin was Alexander the Great, king of Macedonia.

4. Although the digital display on a calculator gives the answer in base 10 form, the actual calculation within the gadget is done by a series of on/off switches according to the base two or binary system. This system is sometimes referred to as Boolean Algebra after mathematician George Boole.

5. Babylon's intellectual King Hammurabi reigned over amazing feats of computation by his mathematicians. However, they had no symbol for zero. By 300 B.C., a symbol for zero had appeared in cuneiform tablets.

6. Around 825 A.D., Al-Khowarizmi of Baghdad popularized the technique of using 10 numerals whose position determined their value, our decimal system.

7. It took nearly two centuries for the decimal system popularized in Baghdad to reach Spain. There it was called Ghobar numerals from the Arabic word for *sand* as sandboxes were occasionally used instead of paper to compute a problem.

8. By the late 13th century, the city-state of Florence, Italy, was passing laws against the dangerous "decimals." This was to protect honest citizens against bank forgers who could easily change amounts by tampering with a 0, 6 or 9.

9. Al-Kashi, the 15th century director of the astronomical observatory at Samarkand, was one of the first to realize that fractions could be written as decimals and computation would be easier.

TENTHS

Directions: Circle the correct fraction for the shaded area.

1.   ¹/₂   ²/₃   ³/₂

2. 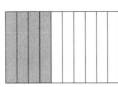   ⁴/₆   ⁶/₁₀   ⁴/₁₀

Directions: Write the fraction for each shaded area.

3.   = _____

4.    = _____

Directions: Write the decimal for each fraction.

5. ⁵/₁₀ = _____   1²/₁₀ = _____   3⁹/₁₀ = _____   2⁷/₁₀ = _____   1⁹/₁₀ = _____   2⁴/₁₀ = _____

Directions: Write the decimal for each.

6. two and four tenths = _____

    five and nine tenths = _____

    nine and five tenths = _____

Directions: Write each fraction in words.

7. 1⁹/₁₀ = _____

    _____

    3⁷/₁₀ = _____

    _____

CHALLENGE:

Connect the dots in order from smallest to largest.
Then draw from the largest back to the smallest.

1.1

1.6   2.5

3.1   1.3

1.2   4.2

2.2

Name _____

TENTHS

Directions: Write the fraction for the shaded area.

1.   = _____

2.   = _____

Directions: Write the decimal for each fraction.

3. $\frac{9}{10}$ = _____   4. $1\frac{4}{10}$ = _____   5. $3\frac{8}{10}$ = _____

6. $8\frac{3}{10}$ = _____   7. $12\frac{2}{10}$ = _____   8. $5\frac{5}{10}$ = _____

Directions: Write the decimal for each.

9. one and two tenths = _____

   two and one tenth = _____

   three and nine tenths = _____

   eight and five tenths = _____

Directions: Write each fraction in words.

10. $7\frac{5}{10}$ = _____

    _____

    $5\frac{7}{10}$ = _____

    _____

    $8\frac{3}{10}$ = _____

    _____

CHALLENGE:

Answer with a decimal. What part of the figure is:

black _____
gray _____
white _____
not black _____
not white _____
not gray _____

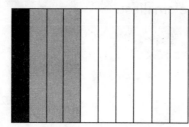

INTRODUCTION: Remind students that when a fraction has a denominator of 10, it can be written as a decimal.

$$5/10 = .5$$

Show them the activity page "Unit with Tenths" (page 12) in a page protector with $5/10$ colored.

HUNDREDTHS: Then show them the "Unit with Hundredths" activity page (page 17) in a page protector with $50/100$ colored. Put both fractions on the board.

$$50/100 = 5/10 = .5$$

We now add the second number after the decimal to talk about hundredths.

$$50/100 = .50$$

This is read 50 hundredths.

(If students do not remember how to reduce $50/100$ to $5/10$, use the *Math Phonics™–Fractions* book to explain this to them.)

If we colored in 53 of the small squares, we would have

$$53/100 = .53$$

For only three of the hundredths, we would have $3/100 = .03$

This is read three hundredths.

OPTIONAL: Give each student "Unit with Hundredths" (page 17), a vinyl page protector, a crayon and a facial tissue. Ask groups of students to color in a decimal fraction such as .15, .23, .46, etc. Have each student write each number as a fraction and as a decimal.

REVIEWING PLACE VALUE: Put this number on the board: 530.48

Ask the place value of each number and make a place value chart for students to think about.

5	3	0 .	4	8
hundreds	tens	ones	tenths	hundredths

Sometimes we hear this number read as five hundred *and* thirty and forty-eight hundredths. The correct way to read it is only to use the word *and* when you come to the decimal point. This helps avoid confusion. Read this number.

  five hundred thirty and forty-eight hundredths

Be sure students notice the difference between *tens* and *tenths* and between *hundreds* and *hundredths*. Ask them the difference between one hundred dollars and one hundredth of a dollar. Which one would they rather have?

The *th* on the end of the word means a fractional part or a decimal part of a number. The *th* means the number is to the right of the decimal.

OPTIONAL: Ask students to guess how you might read this number: 2.153

The 1 is in the tenths place, the 5 is in the hundredths place and the 3 is in the thousandths place. It could be written as a fraction: $2^{153}/_{1000}$

Both are read two and one hundred fifty-three thousandths. We will study only tenths and hundredths in this book. We will not study thousandths.

DECIMAL BINGO: After teaching this lesson, you may begin using decimal bingo in your classroom. Refer to the instructions for Decimal Bingo on page 19.

MATH HISTORY TRIVIA: The word *decimal* is based on the Latin word *decimus* meaning "tenth." The decimal system uses 10 numerals—0, 1, 2, 3, 4, 5, 6, 7, 8 and 9. This system was probably developed mainly because each human has 10 fingers. Use the wall chart "Writing One to Ten" on page 18 to teach your students a little math history. This can be enlarged, laminated and posted in the classroom.

UNIT WITH HUNDREDTHS

WRITING ONE TO TEN

BABYLONIAN
(STYLUS ON CLAY)

EGYPTIAN
(PEN ON PAPYRUS)

MAYAN
(STICKS AND PEBBLES)

CHINESE
(PEN ON PAPER)

GREEK
(FROM THEIR ALPHABET LETTERS)

ROMAN
(FROM FINGER COUNTING—V = 5 REPRESENTS THE ANGLE BETWEEN THUMB AND INDEX FINGER)

DECIMAL BINGO FOR BEGINNERS

Use after Lesson Plan 2.

1. Give each student a blank bingo card. Let students write *FREE* in one space, wherever they choose.
2. Write these decimals on the board. Students should pick five decimals from each group and write them at random in the spaces on the card.

   .2   .3   .4   .5   .6   .7   .8   .9

   .02 .03 .04 .05 .06 .07 .08 .09

   .11 .12 .13 .14 .15 .16 .17 .18

3. **Optional.** Laminate each card for durability and so students can use crayon to cross off numbers that are called. This cuts down on classroom clutter from markers to cover numbers during the game.
4. Teacher or leader draws an addition or subtraction card and *calls only the answer*. Students simply cover the decimal on the card. Four in a row gives a bingo.

DECIMAL BINGO—ADDITION AND SUBTRACTION

Use after Lesson Plan 4.

Follow steps one, two and three.

For step four, draw an addition or subtraction card. Read the problem and students must figure the answer in their heads or on scratch paper and cover the answer on the card.

DECIMAL BINGO—MULTIPLICATION AND DIVISION

Use after Lesson Plan 7.

Follow steps one, two and three.

For step four, draw a multiplication or division card. Read the problem and students must figure the answer in their heads or on scratch paper and cover the answer on the card.

Optional: Make your own set of problem cards using the blank problem cards on pages 22 and 23. Make the problems harder, but use the same answers to save having to make a new set of cards.

Prizes: These are optional. If you do not want to worry about keeping prizes in your classroom, the "prize" could be that all who bingo could leave class a few seconds before everyone else. If you want to give an object to those who bingo, ask parents to donate pencils, erasers, stickers, etc.

$.2 + .3 = .5$	$.2 + .7 = .9$	$.09 - .04 = .05$	$.03 + .06 = .09$	$.17 - .03 = .14$
$.5 - .1 = .4$	$.3 + .5 = .8$	$.07 - .03 = .04$	$.05 + .03 = .08$	$.19 - .06 = .13$
$.1 + .2 = .3$	$.9 - .2 = .7$	$.09 - .06 = .03$	$.06 + .01 = .07$	$.15 - .03 = .12$
$.1 + .1 = .2$	$.8 - .2 = .6$	$.07 - .05 = .02$	$.04 + .02 = .06$	$.18 - .07 = .11$

BINGO DRAWING CARDS

.15 + .03 = .18	$5\overline{)2.5}$ = .5	$3\overline{)2.7}$ = .9	$5\overline{).25}$ = .05	.3 x .3 = .09
.08 + .09 = .17	2 x .2 = .4	.4 x 2 = .8	.2 x .2 = .04	.4 x .2 = .08
.11 + .05 = .16	.05 x 6 = .30 or .3	$2\overline{)1.4}$ = .7	$3\overline{).09}$ = .03	$4\overline{).28}$ = .07
.09 + .06 = .15	.1 x 2 = .2	$6\overline{)3.6}$ = .6	$2\overline{).04}$ = .02	.2 x .3 = .06

$5\overline{)\,.70}$ = .14

.3 x .6 = .18

$4\overline{)\,.52}$ = .13

$2\overline{)\,.34}$ = .17

$3\overline{)\,.36}$ = .12

.8 x .2 = .16

$2\overline{)\,.22}$ = .11

.3 x .5 = .15

BINGO DRAWING CARDS

Name _____

HUNDREDTHS

Directions: Write the decimal for each.

1. $48/100$ = _____

2. $73/100$ = _____

3. $4/100$ = _____

4. $40/100$ = _____

5. $18/100$ = _____

6. $7/100$ = _____

Directions: Write each decimal.

7. one and two tenths = _____

8. ten and twenty-one hundredths = _____

9. one and two hundredths = _____

10. fifteen and twenty-five hundredths = _____

Directions: Write each decimal in words.

11. 5.5 =

12. 50.05 =

13. 250.50 =

14. 50.15 =

15. 15.50 =

15.50

5.5   50.05

CHALLENGE:

Build a number.

6 in the hundredths place

7 in the tens place

5 in the ones place

3 in the hundreds place

9 in the tenths place

What is the number ? _____

HUNDREDTHS

PLACE VALUE CHART

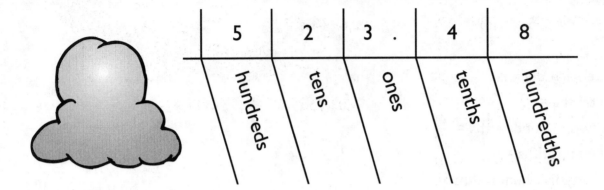

5	2	3	.	4	8
hundreds	tens	ones		tenths	hundredths

In this number what is the value of the:

5 = 5 hundreds = 500

2 = _____ = _____

3 = _____ = _____

4 = _____ = _____

8 = _____ = _____

Directions: Write each number.

1. 5 in tenths place, 4 in ones place = _____

2. 4 in hundreds place, 2 in ones place, 3 in tenths place = _____

3. 8 in ones place, 5 in hundredths place, 2 in tenths place = _____

4. 4 in hundreds place, 4 in hundredths place = _____

Directions: Write the decimal for each fraction.

5. $15\frac{5}{10}$ = _____

6. $35\frac{5}{100}$ = _____

7. $154\frac{5}{10}$ = _____

CHALLENGE:

If you have two dimes, three pennies and two quarters, what fractional part of a dollar do you have? _____ Write as a decimal _____

INTRODUCTION: Another way to understand decimals is to think of money. Since there are 100 cents in a dollar, one penny is $1/100$ or .01 of a dollar. We write one penny as $.01 and call it one cent or one penny. The word *cent* is based on the Latin word *centum* meaning "hundred." Ask students if they can think of any other words with **cent** in them. Some answers might be *century* which means "one hundred years" or *centimeter* which means "one hundredth of a meter." When we talk about percent, we are talking about a certain amount out of a hundred or per hundred or percent.

MONEY AS A DECIMAL:

 = $1/100$ = .01 = $.01

 = $5/100$ = .05 = $.05

 = $10/100$ = .10 = $.10

 = $25/100$ = .25 = $.25

 = $50/100$ = .50 = $.50

 = $100/100$ = 1.00 = $1.00

COINS AS FRACTIONS: Take another look at the 25-cent piece. What do you get when you reduce $25/100$?

$$25/100 = 5/20 = 1/4$$

We know that four of these coins will equal one dollar, and looking at the fraction shows why. *Quarter* means "fourth"–that's why a 25-cent piece is sometimes called a quarter.

Look at a 50-cent piece as a fraction of a dollar.

$$50/100 = 5/10 = 1/2$$

It makes sense to call a 50-cent piece a half-dollar when we look at the fraction.

Look at the nickel as a fraction and reduce.

$$5/100 = 1/20$$

Count by fives to one hundred. How many are there? Twenty. There are 20 nickels in a dollar.

Write the dime as a fraction and reduce.

$$10/100 = 1/10$$

How many dimes in a dollar? Ten.

HOMEWORK: Worksheets E and F (pages 29 and 30). See if the students can figure out the coin problems on Worksheet E. In Lesson Plan 5, there is a method suggested for teaching students to solve this type of problem. This is good practice for some types of algebra problems students will have later.

MATH HISTORY BONUS: A quarter is sometimes referred to as two *bits*. The word comes from a Spanish coin called a "real" or a "bit." Eight of them equalled a dollar.

The first national leader to have his head stamped on a coin was Alexander the Great, king of Macedonia.

LESSON PLAN 4
ADDITION AND SUBTRACTION

ADDING DECIMALS: Use fractions to help students understand how to add and subtract decimals.

Example: .5

             + .6

5 + 6 = 11, but where do you put the decimal? Is the answer 11; 1.1 or .11?

Work it as a fraction problem.

$$\frac{5}{10} + \frac{6}{10} = \frac{11}{10} = 1\frac{1}{10}$$

The decimal answer should be 1.1, also. For decimals, add as usual and keep the decimals in the answer in a straight line with the decimals in the problem.

What about hundredths?

Example: .25

             + .18

Try it as a fraction.

$$\frac{25}{100} + \frac{18}{100} = \frac{43}{100}$$

The decimal answer is .43, the same as the fraction.

INTRODUCTION: Review tenths and hundredths.

$$\text{one tenth} = \frac{1}{10} = .1$$

$$\text{one hundredth} = \frac{1}{100} = .01$$

Give your class the assessment pages for addition and subtraction (pages 43 and 45). For those who need help, use *Math Phonics™– Addition* and *Math Phonics™–Subtraction* books for worksheets, study sheets, etc.

Students must be able to add and subtract correctly to be able to work with decimals.

SUBTRACTING DECIMALS: Try this decimal problem:

$$1.3$$

$$- .8$$

Work it as a fraction problem.

$$1\frac{3}{10} - \frac{8}{10} = \frac{13}{10} - \frac{8}{10} = \frac{5}{10}$$

The decimal answer is .5, also. (Which is easier?) There are fewer numbers to write for decimals.

For subtraction of fractions, subtract as usual and take the decimal straight down.

DECIMALS WALL CHART: Make a copy of the wall chart on page 33 for each student. Students should keep the chart in their math folder or take home to post on a wall or mirror. All wall charts can be enlarged and laminated and posted in the classroom.

NOTES TO PARENTS: Send home notes to parents (page 34) at appropriate times.

KEY WORDS IN PROBLEM SOLVING: Talk a little bit about these key words when you are ready to assign Worksheet I (page 40). Give each student a copy of Wall Chart C (page 37) for math folders. Go over the first two problems in class. Point out that some word problems have several key words in them. Usually, the key word in the last sentence is the one that tells whether to add, subtract, multiply or divide. Have students read all the problems on Worksheet H (page 39) and write one of the four process words. Check in class to see that they have the right process. Then assign them to find all the answers as a homework assignment.

MAGIC SQUARES: A magic square is a 3 x 3 array of numbers in which each row–vertical, horizontal and diagonal–has the same sum. Show the class this start of a magic square.

The magic number is 27.

	5	12
	9	
	13	

We can add the three numbers in the center vertical row and see that the sum is 27. The magic number for this square is 27. Now help the class find the other numbers to make sums of 27 by adding and subtracting. (9 + 12 = 21; 27 - 21 = 6; 6 goes in the lower left corner)

LEVEL 2: Starting with this lesson, there will be a level II worksheet included with each set of pages. Teachers could use this for advanced students when most of the class needs to do another basic page. Also, if you are teaching from this book as a review of material already studied, Level 2 pages work well.

DECIMAL BINGO FOR ADDITION AND SUBTRACTION: After you have taught this lesson, teach the class Decimal Bingo for Addition and Subtraction (page 19).

FLASH CARDS: Copy the tenths and hundredths flash cards (pages 35 and 36) on card stock for each student. This game can be played for addition or subtraction, one or two players.

ONE-PLAYER FLASH CARDS: Divide the cards into two piles facedown. Turn up the two top cards. Give the sum or difference. Check by doing the problem on scratch paper.

TWO-PLAYER FLASH CARDS: Deal cards to the two players. Place cards facedown. Each player turns up the top card. Decide ahead of time whether to add or subtract. The first one to give the correct answer gets both cards. When one player runs out of cards, the other is the winner. If players are evenly matched, count cards after five minutes. Player with the most cards wins.

MATH HISTORY BONUS: Although the digital display on a calculator gives the answer in base 10 form, the actual calculation within the gadget is done by a series of on/off switches according to the base two or binary system. This system is sometimes referred to as Boolean Algebra after mathematician George Boole.

DECIMALS

DECIMALS ARE EASIER WAYS OF WRITING
FRACTIONS WITH DENOMINATORS OF 10 OR 100

 = $^1/_{10}$ = .1

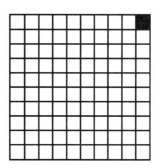 = $^1/_{100}$ = .01

ADDING AND SUBTRACTING DECIMALS

KEEP DECIMALS IN A STRAIGHT LINE

$^1/_{10} + {}^3/_{10} = {}^4/_{10}$

$$\begin{array}{r} .1 \\ +\ .3 \\ \hline .4 \end{array}$$

ADD ZEROS IF NECESSARY

3.6 + 4.21 = ?

$$\begin{array}{r} 3.60 \\ +\ 4.21 \\ \hline 7.81 \end{array}$$

PARENTS' NOTES

Dear Parents,

We are beginning our unit on decimals, and we will need some support from you at home. We will use the *Math Phonics™–Decimals* system, and we will be sending home several wall charts which should be posted at home. Please help your child find a good place for these charts where they will be seen several times every day. The bathroom mirror, the light switch in the bedroom or the side of the fridge may be some good spots.

Quiz your child verbally two or three times about the material on each chart until you think he or she has learned it.

Thanks for your help!

Sincerely,

Dear Parents,

In _____ days we will take an assessment or quiz about the basic addition and subtraction facts. Please review these with your child. Students must know these facts in order to learn about decimals!

Thanks for your help!

Sincerely,

KEY WORDS IN PROBLEM SOLVING

ADD
SUM
TOTAL
IN ALL
TOGETHER
PERIMETER
DISTANCE AROUND

SUBTRACT
LESS
MORE
CHANGE
REMAINDER
SALE PRICE
DIFFERENCE
HOW MUCH TALLER
HOW MUCH IS LEFT
HOW MANY WERE SOLD

MULTIPLY
AREA
TOTAL
FACTORS
PRODUCTS
OF MEANS "TIMES"
TIMES MEANS "OF"

DIVIDE
EACH
APIECE
AVERAGE
QUOTIENT
PER PERSON
FOR EACH ONE
HOW MUCH FOR ONE

ADDING AND SUBTRACTING

Directions: Add.

1. .7	2. 1.8	3. 3.5	4. 4.9	5. 9.8
+ .2	+ 1.1	+ 2.7	+ 7.4	+ 5.9

Directions: Subtract.

6. .9	7. 2.4	8. 5.7	9. 9.8	10. 6.3
- .3	- .8	- 3.8	- 7.9	- 5.8

Directions: Add.

11. .93	12. .48	13. 1.69	14. 5.17	15. 9.08
+ .06	+ .25	+ 2.73	+ 3.94	+ 7.36

Directions: Subtract.

16. .28	17. .69	18. .32	19. 5.61	20. 7.23
- .13	- .43	- .28	- 2.48	- 2.48

21. When your brother bought his new car, the odometer read 335.8 miles. Now it reads 986.1 miles. How many miles have been put on the car since he bought it? _____

22. Normal body temperature is 98.6 degrees. When your teacher had the flu, she had 3.9 degrees above normal. What was her total temperature when she was sick? _____

CHALLENGE:

Find the magic number by adding the three diagonal numbers. Every row, column and diagonal will equal the same magic number. Find all the missing numbers.

Magic Number

_____

.6		.8
	.5	
.2		

Name _____

FINDING KEY WORDS

Directions: For each problem, find key words and write *add*, *subtract*, *multiply* or *divide* on the first line. Then find the answer and write it on the second line.

_____ 1. Your friend's yard is a square measuring 81.5 feet on each side. What is the total
_____   distance around the yard?

_____ 2. The two best hitters on the softball team have batting averages of .325 and .318.
_____   What is the difference between these two averages?

_____ 3. You are 66.5 inches tall and your teacher is 69.8 inches tall. How much taller is your
_____   teacher?

_____ 4. You and your friends have saved $10.25; $16.80 and $25.20 towards your trip. What
_____   is the amount saved in all?

_____ 5. Twelve people have eaten 48 pieces of candy in all. What is the average number of
_____   pieces that each person ate?

_____ 6. If it rained 4.28 inches today and it rained 2.19 inches yesterday, how much more
_____   rain fell today than yesterday?

_____ 7. Your teacher bought 9 books for $81.00. What was the average cost of each one?
_____

_____ 8. If you had $10.50 and spent $7.95, how much change would you get?
_____

_____ 9. Six people in your class each spent four dollars on lunch. What was the total amount
_____   of money spent by those people?

_____ 10. Your time for the 100-yard dash is 11.9 seconds and the school record is 10.8
_____   seconds. How much more is your time?

CHALLENGE:

Find the missing numbers in this magic square.

Magic Number:

_____

.15		
	.30	
	.10	.45

Name _____

WORKSHEET 1

ADDITION AND SUBTRACTION

Directions: Add.

1. 58.3 + 31.0	2. 0.53 + 0.99	3. 2.6 + 3.7	4. 0.74 + 0.84	5. 89.2 + 76.9

Directions: Subtract.

6. 7.5 - 6.8	7. 0.83 - 0.37	8. 269.2 - 138.8	9. 582.0 - 394.8	10. 635.8 - 256.9

Directions: Add or subtract.

11. .39 + .87	12. 27.2 - 19.8	13. 6.54 - 3.27	14. 22.95 + 14.33	15. 93.82 + 24.76

16. 72.8 - 6.9	17. 389.6 - 126.9	18. 293.0 + 183.8	19. 215.23 + 27.46	20. 622.93 - 98.79

21. You have a one dollar bill, six quarters, five nickels and five dimes. Do you have enough to buy three 95¢ sodas (tax included)? _____ How much change will you get back? _____

22. I'm thinking of a number. When you double the number and add .5, you have (7.5). What is the number? _____

CHALLENGE:

In working with your calculator, you discover that two of the numbers are not working right. You realize that when you push the button marked 4, the calculator really adds 3. When you add these decimals: .4 + .5 + .5 + .4 + .4 + .5 + .5, you get 3.2 which is the right answer.

What does the calculator add when you punch the .5? _____

40   **LEVEL 2**

SUMMARY OF RULES

ADDITION RULES

EVENS AND ODDS: An even number always ends in 0, 2, 4, 6 or 8.

An odd number always ends in 1, 3, 5, 7 or 9.

0s: When you add zero to a number, the number stays the same. (4 + 0 = 4)

1s: When you add one to a number, the answer is the next number on the number line. (5 + 1 = 6)

2s: When adding two to an even number, the answer is the next even number. (4 + 2 = 6, 6 + 2 = 8)

When adding two to an odd number, the answer is the next odd number. (3 + 2 = 5, 5 + 2 = 7)

DOUBLES: Answers to the doubles (2 + 2, 3 + 3, etc.) are always even.

NUMBER NEIGHBORS: Number neighbors are any two numbers side-by-side on the number line. (Ex: 5 and 6 or 6 and 7)

When you add two number neighbors, the answer is always an odd number. (Ex: 5 + 6 = 11, 6 + 7 = 13). To add two number neighbors, double the smaller number and add 1. (Since 5 + 5 = 10, you know 5 + 6 = 11.)

Whenever you add an even and an odd number, the answer is an odd number. (3 + 6 = 9, 7 + 8 = 15)

9s: To add nine to a number, first subtract one from the number. Then put a 1 in front of that answer. (6 + 9 = 15, 8 + 9 = 17)

SUBTRACTION RULES

NUMBER NEIGHBORS: When you subtract a smaller number neighbor from a larger number neighbor, the answer is always one. (8 - 7 = 1, 9 - 8 = 1)

When you subtract a larger number neighbor from a smaller number neighbor and you can borrow, the answer is nine. (17 - 8 = 9, 15 - 6 = 9)

1s: When you subtract one from a number, the answer is the smaller number neighbor.

9s: When you subtract nine from a teens number, add the numerals of the teens number. That is the answer. (15 - 9 = 6, 13 - 9 = 4)

2s: When you subtract two from an odd number, the answer is the next smaller odd number. (7 - 2 = 5, 9 - 2 = 7)

When you subtract two from an even number, the answer is the next smaller even number. (8 - 2 = 6, 6 - 2 = 4)

When you subtract two closest odd numbers, the answer is two. (7 - 5 = 2, 9 - 7 = 2)

When you subtract two closest even numbers, the answer is two. (8 - 6 = 2, 6 - 4 = 2)

TLC10200 Copyright © Teaching & Learning Company, Carthage, IL 62321-0010

ADDITION FACTS

Zeros

0 + 0 = 0
0 + 1 = 1
0 + 2 = 2
0 + 3 = 3
0 + 4 = 4
0 + 5 = 5
0 + 6 = 6
0 + 7 = 7
0 + 8 = 8
0 + 9 = 9

1s

1 + 1 = 2
1 + 2 = 3
1 + 3 = 4
1 + 4 = 5
1 + 5 = 6
1 + 6 = 7
1 + 7 = 8
1 + 8 = 9
1 + 9 = 10

2s

2 + 2 = 4
2 + 4 = 6
2 + 6 = 8
2 + 8 = 10

2 + 3 = 5
2 + 5 = 7
2 + 7 = 9
2 + 9 = 11

3s

3 + 3 = 6
3 + 4 = 7
3 + 5 = 8
3 + 6 = 9
3 + 7 = 10
3 + 8 = 11
3 + 9 = 12

4s

4 + 4 = 8
4 + 5 = 9
4 + 6 = 10
4 + 7 = 11
4 + 8 = 12
4 + 9 = 13

5s

5 + 5 = 10
5 + 6 = 11
5 + 7 = 12
5 + 8 = 13
5 + 9 = 14

6s

6 + 6 = 12
6 + 7 = 13
6 + 8 = 14
6 + 9 = 15

7s

7 + 7 = 14
7 + 8 = 15
7 + 9 = 16

8s

8 + 8 = 16
8 + 9 = 17

9s

9 + 9 = 18

42

Name _____

ADDITION ASSESSMENT

1. **5** + **4** = _____   2. **3** + **1** = _____   3. **10** + **10** = _____

4. **2** + **0** = _____   5. **5** + **5** = _____   6. **3** + **3** = _____

7. **3** + **2** = _____   8. **6** + **6** = _____   9. **0** + **0** = _____

10. **9** + **4** = _____   11. **1** + **2** = _____   12. **5** + **2** = _____

13. **4** + **0** = _____   14. **1** + **8** = _____   15. **8** + **8** = _____

16. **4** + **3** = _____   17. **9** + **1** = _____   18. **1** + **4** = _____

19. **6** + **3** = _____   20. **0** + **1** = _____   21. **10** + **4** = _____

22. **6** + **5** = _____   23. **0** + **3** = _____   24. **7** + **7** = _____

25. **9** + **8** = _____   26. **8** + **7** = _____   27. **1** + **1** = _____

28. **3** + **7** = _____   29. **5** + **1** = _____   30. **5** + **7** = _____

31. **10** + **3** = _____   32. **4** + **4** = _____   33. **7** + **9** = _____

34. **0** + **5** = _____   35. **8** + **3** = _____   36. **4** + **6** = _____

37. **1** + **6** = _____   38. **6** + **0** = _____   39. **3** + **9** = _____

40. **2** + **6** = _____   41. **7** + **1** = _____   42. **9** + **2** = _____

43. **0** + **7** = _____   44. **2** + **2** = _____   45. **7** + **6** = _____

46. **10** + **8** = _____   47. **2** + **8** = _____   48. **8** + **5** = _____

49. **7** + **2** = _____   50. **7** + **4** = _____   51. **10** + **1** = _____

52. **8** + **0** = _____   53. **5** + **9** = _____   54. **9** + **6** = _____

55. **2** + **4** = _____   56. **0** + **9** = _____   57. **3** + **5** = _____

58. **10** + **5** = _____   59. **10** + **0** = _____   60. **10** + **9** = _____

61. **6** + **8** = _____   62. **4** + **8** = _____   63. **10** + **7** = _____

64. **10** + **6** = _____   65. **10** + **2** = _____   66. **9** + **9** = _____

43

SUBTRACTION FACTS

0s	1s	2s	3s	4s
0 - 0 = 0	1 - 1 = 0	2 - 2 = 0	3 - 3 = 0	4 - 4 = 0
	1 - 0 = 1	2 - 1 = 1	3 - 2 = 1	4 - 3 = 1
		2 - 0 = 2	3 - 1 = 2	4 - 2 = 2
			3 - 0 = 3	4 - 1 = 3
				4 - 0 = 4

5s	6s	7s	8s	9s
5 - 5 = 0	6 - 6 = 0	7 - 7 = 0	8 - 8 = 0	9 - 9 = 0
5 - 4 = 1	6 - 5 = 1	7 - 6 = 1	8 - 7 = 1	9 - 8 = 1
5 - 3 = 2	6 - 4 = 2	7 - 5 = 2	8 - 6 = 2	9 - 7 = 2
5 - 2 = 3	6 - 3 = 3	7 - 4 = 3	8 - 5 = 3	9 - 6 = 3
5 - 1 = 4	6 - 2 = 4	7 - 3 = 4	8 - 4 = 4	9 - 5 = 4
5 - 0 = 5	6 - 1 = 5	7 - 2 = 5	8 - 3 = 5	9 - 4 = 5
	6 - 0 = 6	7 - 1 = 6	8 - 2 = 6	9 - 3 = 6
		7 - 0 = 7	8 - 1 = 7	9 - 2 = 7
			8 - 0 = 8	9 - 1 = 8
				9 - 0 = 9

10s	11s	12s	13s	14s
10 - 9 = 1	11 - 9 = 2	12 - 9 = 3	13 - 9 = 4	14 - 9 = 5
10 - 8 = 2	11 - 8 = 3	12 - 8 = 4	13 - 8 = 5	14 - 8 = 6
10 - 7 = 3	11 - 7 = 4	12 - 7 = 5	13 - 7 = 6	14 - 7 = 7
10 - 6 = 4	11 - 6 = 5	12 - 6 = 6	13 - 6 = 7	14 - 6 = 8
10 - 5 = 5	11 - 5 = 6	12 - 5 = 7	13 - 5 = 8	14 - 5 = 9
10 - 4 = 6	11 - 4 = 7	12 - 4 = 8	13 - 4 = 9	
10 - 3 = 7	11 - 3 = 8	12 - 3 = 9		
10 - 2 = 8	11 - 2 = 9			
10 - 1 = 9				

15s	16s	17s	18s
15 - 9 = 6	16 - 9 = 7	17 - 9 = 8	18 - 9 = 9
15 - 8 = 7	16 - 8 = 8	17 - 8 = 9	
15 - 7 = 8	16 - 7 = 9		
15 - 6 = 9			

Notice that starting with the 10s, we do not include 10 - 10 = 0, 11 - 11 = 0, 11 - 10 = 1 and so on. The reason is that students have already had 1 - 1 = 0 and 0 - 0 = 0, so there is no need to repeat those with the 10s, 11s and larger numbers.

TLC10200 Copyright © Teaching & Learning Company, Carthage, IL 62321-0010

SUBTRACTION ASSESSMENT

| 1. 7
 - 6 | 2. 11
 - 2 | 3. 4
 - 3 | 4. 8
 - 7 | 5. 9
 - 4 | 6. 5
 - 0 | 7. 10
 -10 | 8. 16
 - 8 | 9. 11
 - 8 |

| 10. 12
 - 6 | 11. 10
 - 9 | 12. 14
 - 5 | 13. 11
 - 5 | 14. 10
 - 8 | 15. 15
 - 7 | 16. 10
 - 7 | 17. 8
 - 8 | 18. 7
 - 7 |

| 19. 8
 - 4 | 20. 8
 - 1 | 21. 13
 - 6 | 22. 11
 - 6 | 23. 7
 - 5 | 24. 11
 - 7 | 25. 2
 - 0 | 26. 9
 - 3 | 27. 4
 - 1 |

| 28. 1
 - 1 | 29. 12
 - 8 | 30. 16
 - 9 | 31. 13
 - 8 | 32. 6
 - 6 | 33. 3
 - 0 | 34. 15
 - 9 | 35. 13
 - 7 | 36. 6
 - 1 |

| 37. 12
 - 3 | 38. 5
 - 4 | 39. 14
 - 7 | 40. 6
 - 3 | 41. 10
 - 6 | 42. 9
 - 0 | 43. 14
 - 8 | 44. 13
 - 9 | 45. 8
 - 0 |

| 46. 12
 - 9 | 47. 9
 - 9 | 48. 5
 - 2 | 49. 11
 - 7 | 50. 11
 - 3 | 51. 15
 - 6 | 52. 9
 - 8 | 53. 11
 - 9 | 54. 10
 - 2 |

| 55. 5
 - 3 | 56. 5
 - 5 | 57. 3
 - 3 | 58. 16
 - 7 | 59. 9
 - 1 | 60. 12
 - 7 | 61. 6
 - 0 | 62. 4
 - 0 | 63. 10
 - 1 |

| 64. 5
 - 1 | 65. 7
 - 1 | 66. 10
 - 4 | 67. 15
 - 8 | 68. 12
 - 1 | 69. 9
 - 6 | 70. 8
 - 3 | 71. 2
 - 1 | 72. 3
 - 2 |

| 73. 14
 - 9 | 74. 18
 - 9 | 75. 17
 - 8 | 76. 6
 - 4 | 77. 0
 - 0 | 78. 7
 - 4 | 79. 6
 - 2 | 80. 10
 - 3 | 81. 7
 - 0 |

| 82. 9
 - 8 | 83. 13
 - 4 | 84. 9
 - 4 | 85. 17
 - 9 | 86. 10
 - 5 | 87. 6
 - 5 | 88. 12
 - 4 | 89. 1
 - 0 | 90. 7
 - 3 |

| 91. 9
 - 7 | 92. 2
 - 2 | 93. 14
 - 6 | 94. 13
 - 5 | 95. 8
 - 5 | 96. 3
 - 1 | 97. 4
 - 4 | 98. 8
 - 2 | 99. 4
 - 2 |

| 100. 8
 - 6 | 101. 7
 - 2 |

INTRODUCTION: Which is larger 36 or 36.0?

They are the same. Ask the class why. Both numbers have 3 tens, 6 ones and no tenths.

What about 21.5 and 21.50?

Ask the class why they are equal. It is because both have 21 in the whole numbers, and .5 and .50 are both equal to $1/2$. $.5 = {}^5/_{10} = {}^1/_2$ $.50 = {}^{50}/_{100} = {}^1/_2$

ADDITION: If you needed to add 36.1 + 41.42, it could be written this way:

$$\begin{array}{r} 36.1 \\ + \ 41.42 \\ \hline \end{array}$$

but then you would be adding .1 and .02 which is the same as 1/10 and 2/100 and they do not have common denominators. We would write the problem as 36.10 + 41.42 and then be adding common denominators.

$$\begin{array}{r} 36.10 \\ + \ 41.42 \\ \hline 77.52 \end{array}$$

Now tenths are added to tenths and hundredths are added to hundredths.

EXAMPLES: Ask students how they would do this problem:
3.5 + 4.06 = ?

$$\begin{array}{r} 3.50 \\ + \ 4.06 \\ \hline 7.56 \end{array}$$

Also keep decimals in a straight line for subtraction to subtract common denominators.

Give the class some examples.   4.5 - 2 =

26.3 - 12.15 =

MAGIC SQUARES: Talk about magic squares. Copy the directions for making your own magic square on page 52 for each student. Worksheet M (page 51) can be used as a Level 2 worksheet or it can be assigned to all students.

SOLVING COIN PROBLEMS: This is very easy for some students and seems impossible for others. Here is a method that all can learn and use. Make a chart. We will use 16¢ because that is like the problem for Worksheet K (page 49).

Pennies	Nickels	Dimes	
1	1	1	= 3 coins
6		1	= 7 coins

Have students find all the different ways coins can equal 16¢. If the problem asked for four coins, you look at your chart to find which combination has four coins. It is one penny and three nickels.

COLORED QUILT BLOCK: Worksheet L (page 50) can be used as an in-class activity page or as an assignment.

MATH HISTORY BONUS: Babylon's intellectual King Hammurabi reigned over amazing feats of computation by his mathematicians. However, they had no symbol for zero. By 300 B.C., a symbol for zero had appeared in cuneiform tablets.

Ask students to devise a way to write these numbers if zero did not exist:

10   105   1005

(There could be an X or an empty space in place of the zero. Students may think of others.)

1X   1_   1X5   1_5   1XX5   1__5

LINING UP DECIMALS

Directions: Write each problem in a column and add.

    1. 3 + 4.2 = _____   2. 6.1 + 5.13 = _____   3. 10.98 + 5 = _____

Directions: Write each problem in columns and subtract.

    4. 5 - 3.8 = _____   5. 12.38 - 9.2 = _____   6. 8.3 - .09 = _____

Directions: Write each problem in columns and add or subtract.

    7. 39.6 + 22 = _____   8. 31.5 + 0.29 = _____

    9. 22 - 17.38 = _____   10. 0.06 + 24.8 = _____

    11. 3.2 - 2.54 = _____   12. 92 - 25.48 = _____

CHALLENGE:

How many different ways could you make 19¢ in coins? _____

What groups of coins would you use? _____

_____

_____

Pennies	Nickels	Dimes

INTRODUCTION: Remind students that multiplication is the short way of adding the same number several times. We know that 3 x 4 = three groups of four = 4 + 4 + 4 = 12

Remembering this will help with multiplying decimals.

NOTE: When a number has one numeral after the decimal, we say it has one decimal place. If there are two numerals after the decimal, the number has two decimal places.

MULTIPLICATION: Show students this problem:

$$.3$$
$$\underline{x\ 5}$$

We know that 3 x 5 = 15, but where is the decimal? Is it 15 or 1.5 or .15?

As we saw in the introduction, we can add .3 five times to get the correct answer.

$$.3$$
$$.3$$
$$.3$$
$$.3$$
$$\underline{+\ .3}$$
$$1.5$$

We can also work the problem as a fraction problem.

$$^3/_{10} \times {}^5/_1 = {}^{15}/_{10} = 1{}^5/_{10}$$

We have shown two different ways that .3 x 5 = 1.5.

Show the students this problem:

$$.7$$
$$\underline{x\ .4}$$

If you work this as a fraction, it is

$$^7/_{10} \times {}^4/_{10} = {}^{28}/_{100}$$

As a decimal, .28 would be the answer. We can do these problems without having to write them as fractions or writing .3 five times. Ask the students if they can see an easy way to put the decimal in the correct place.

The answer is to count decimal places in the problem. Put the same number of decimal places in the answer.

.3	= 1 decimal place
x 5	
1.5	= 1 decimal place
.7	= 1 decimal place
x .4	= 1 decimal place
.28	= 2 decimal places

Give each student a copy of Wall Chart D (page 55) to remind them of this shortcut.

Try two more examples:

1.2	.14
x 3	x 2

LESSON PLAN 6
CONTINUED

NOTE TO PARENTS: Send home note 3 on page 59.

MULTIPLICATION RULES AND FACTS: Give students copies of pages 60-62 to study. Give the assessment (pages 63 and 64) to check students' knowledge.

HOMEWORK: The Challenge on Worksheet N (page 56) is easy to learn and will give students something fun to try on parents or friends.

MATH HISTORY BONUS: Around 825 A.D., Al-Khowarizmi of Baghdad popularized the technique of using 10 numerals whose position determined their value, our decimal system.

MULTIPLYING DECIMALS

$$\frac{5}{10} \times \frac{6}{10} = \frac{30}{100}$$

$$\begin{array}{r} .5 \\ \times .6 \\ \hline .30 \end{array}$$

COUNT DECIMAL PLACES*

.5 = 1 DECIMAL PLACE
X .6 = + 1 DECIMAL PLACE
.30 = 2 DECIMAL PLACES

ANSWER SHOULD HAVE TOTAL DECIMAL PLACES
WHICH ARE FOUND IN THE PROBLEM

DIVIDING DECIMALS

1. DIVIDING BY A WHOLE NUMBER, PUT DECIMAL DIRECTLY ABOVE DECIMAL INSIDE THE BRACKET.

$$\begin{array}{r} .51 \\ 5 \overline{\smash{)}2.55} \end{array}$$

2. DIVIDING BY A DECIMAL—MOVE DECIMAL TO THE RIGHT OF DIVISOR. MOVE DECIMAL IN BRACKET THE SAME NUMBER OF PLACES. THEN DIVIDE.

$$\begin{array}{r} 33. \\ .3 \overline{\smash{)}9.9} \end{array}$$

***ONE NUMBER AFTER THE DECIMAL = 1 DECIMAL PLACE
TWO NUMBERS AFTER THE DECIMAL = 2 DECIMAL PLACES**

MULTIPLYING DECIMALS

Directions: Put the decimal point in the correct place in these answers.

1.	1.3	2.	42	3.	0.28	4.	27.6	5.	0.16	6.	54
	x 3		x .2		x 3		x .2		x 4		x .06
	39		84		84		552		64		324

Directions: Multiply.

7.	.2	8.	.04	9.	.09	10.	.8	11.	10	12.	100
	x 4		x 3		x 6		x .7		x .56		x .56

Directions: Write in columns and add. Keep decimals in a straight line.

13. 25.3 + 16.01 + 10.8 = _____

14. 17.98 + 35.8 + 6.09 = _____

15. The distance from your home to the store is 2.7 kilometers. If you make one trip each way, how far do you travel? _____

16. You have three extension cords. Each one is 5.2 feet long. How far will they reach when they are all connected? _____

CHALLENGE:

Guessing ages.

1. Pick a number between 1 and 9. Write it as a decimal in the tenths place. _____

2. Multiply the number by 20. _____

3. Add 5. _____

4. Multiply by 50. _____

5. Add your age. _____

6. Subtract 250. _____

The last two digits are your age. The first digit is the number you chose. _____

MULTIPLYING DECIMALS

Directions:

1. Find each answer on another sheet of paper. Color each section that has hundredths in the answer.

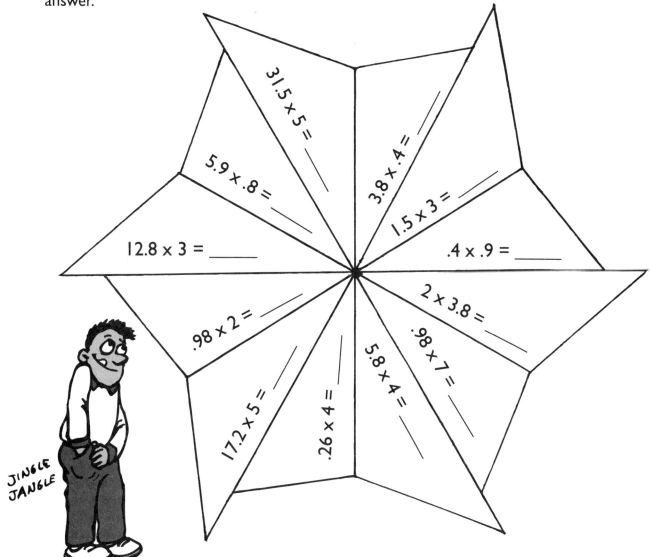

31.5 x 5 =

5.9 x .8 =

12.8 x 3 =

.98 x 2 =

17.2 x 5 =

.26 x 4 =

5.8 x 4 =

.98 x 7 =

2 x 3.8 =

.4 x .9 =

1.5 x 3 =

3.8 x .4 =

JINGLE JANGLE

2. You have 14 coins in your pocket totaling 95¢. How many pennies, dimes and quarters would you need for this amount? _____

3. You are able to jog 7.8 miles in one hour. If you jog for .5 of a hour, how far will you jog?

_____

CHALLENGE:

It is 240,000 miles from the Earth to the moon. If one mile equals 1.6 kilometers, how many kilometers is it from the Earth to the moon? _____

MULTIPLYING DECIMALS

Directions: Your uncle is making an end table modeled after this replica stagecoach. Each dimension will be 3.5 times as large as the small stagecoach. Find the dimensions of the end table.

	Model Stagecoach	End Table
length	5.25"	
height	4"	
width	3"	
door height	3.2"	
door width	.8"	
rear wheel diameter	3.5"	
front wheel diameter	2.5"	
wheel base	5.5"	
axle length	2.8"	
window width	.75"	

Gravity Chart

Earth = 1.0	Moon = .16	Mercury = .38
Venus = .9	Mars = .38	Jupiter = 2.87	Neptune = 1.23
Uranus = .93	Saturn = 1.32	Pluto = .03

According to this chart, if a 100-pound earthling traveled to Neptune, he would weigh 123 pounds (100 x 1.23).

1. How much would an 8-ounce burger weigh on Mercury? _____ On Jupiter? _____

2. How much would a 50-pound earthling weigh on the moon? _____ On Venus? _____

CHALLENGE:

If you weigh 287 pounds on Jupiter, how much would you weigh on Earth? _____

LEVEL 2

PARENTS' NOTES

Dear Parents,

The class will have a review quiz of multiplication facts on _____.
Please help your child study the facts which are on the study sheet.

Go over the study sheets and wall charts which have been sent home in the past. Students need to remember what has been learned earlier because all the information will be used in the study of decimals.

Students also need to memorize the page of multiples so that they can list each group easily.

Thanks for your help!

Sincerely,

Dear Parents,

We will have an assessment of division facts on _____. Please help your child study these facts before the assessment.

Once again, thanks for working with your child at home. The one-on-one math study is extremely valuable for your child.

Sincerely,

P.S. Our class has learned how to play decimal flash cards. Ask your child how to play the game. Although this is a game, it is a very good way for students to practice decimals. I hope you will play this and other math games several times a week. Students do best in math when they have several different ways of learning.

MULTIPLES AND MULTIPLICATION RULES

MULTIPLES

2s: 2, 4, 6, 8, 10, 12, 14, 16, 18, 20

4s: 4, 8, 12, 16, 20, 24, 28, 32, 36, 40

6s: 6, 12, 18, 24, 30, 36, 42, 48, 54, 60

8s: 8, 16, 24, 32, 40, 48, 56, 64, 72, 80

10s: 10, 20, 30, 40, 50, 60, 70, 80, 90, 100

12s: 12, 24, 36, 48, 60, 72, 84, 96, 108, 120

3s: 3, 6, 9, 12, 15, 18, 21, 24, 27, 30

5s: 5, 10, 15, 20, 25, 30, 35, 40, 45, 50

7s: 7, 14, 21, 28, 35, 42, 49, 56, 63, 70

9s: 9, 18, 27, 36, 45, 54, 63, 72, 81, 90

11s: 11, 22, 33, 44, 55, 66, 77, 88, 99, 110

MULTIPLICATION RULES

0s: Any number times 0 equals 0.

1s: Any number times 1 equals that same number.

2s: Any number times 2 is that number added to itself—the doubles in addition. All answers are even.

3s: Memorize answers by learning to count by three.

4s: All answers are even numbers. Answers have a repeating pattern.

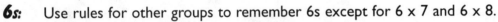

   4   8 12 16 20

24 28 32 36 40

5s: Five times an odd number ends in 5. Five times an even number ends in 0. When multiplying 5 times an even number, take half of the even number and add a zero.

Example: $5 \times 8 = ?$ Half of 8 is 4—the answer is 40.

6s: Use rules for other groups to remember 6s except for 6×7 and 6×8.

Recall $6 \times 6 = 36$

Add another group of 6 $\underline{+\ 6}$

                           $6 \times 7 = 42$

Add another group of 6 $\underline{+\ 6}$

                           $6 \times 8 = 48$

7s: All are learned with other groups except 7×8. Learn this rule: 5, 6, 7, 8 or 56 = 7×8

8s: Use rules from other groups to remember 8s. Answers have repeating numerals in the 1s place.

   8 16 24 32 40

 48 56 64 72 80

9s: Nines answers are in pairs. 18 and 81, 27 and 72, 36 and 63, 45 and 54.

The number in the 10s place is one less than the number you are multiplying by 9. ($9 \times 3 = 27$, $9 \times 4 = 36$)

Numerals in one answer can be added together to equal 9. (18, 1 + 8 = 9; 27, 2 + 7 = 9; etc.)

Here is a rhyme:

When multiplying 9, keep this in mind: Look at a number in the answer line. Add the numerals together. They will equal nine.

10s: Add a zero to the right of the number. (Ex: $3 \times 10 = 30$)

11s: For a one-digit number, write that number in the 10s place and in the 1s place.

12s: For a one-digit number, write that number times 11 and then add that first number.

Ex: $7 \times 12 = \ ?$

              $7 \times 11 = 77$

Add 7 $\underline{+\ 7}$

              $7 \times 12 = 84$

MULTIPLICATION FACTS

Take time to memorize the squares as a group.

```
 0 x  0 =   0
 1 x  1 =   1
 2 x  2 =   4
 3 x  3 =   9
 4 x  4 =  16
 5 x  5 =  25
 6 x  6 =  36
 7 x  7 =  49
 8 x  8 =  64
 9 x  9 =  81
10 x 10 = 100
```

The squares are extremely important in algebra and trigonometry. Some teachers even require students to memorize the squares up to 25 x 25 = 625 to help in solving quadratic equations and trigonometry problems.

Also, notice these patterns in the 9s.

```
 0 x 9 =  0
 1 x 9 =  9
 2 x 9 = 18
 3 x 9 = 27
 4 x 9 = 36
 5 x 9 = 45
 6 x 9 = 54
 7 x 9 = 63
 8 x 9 = 72
 9 x 9 = 81
10 x 9 = 90
```

For the answers 18 through 90, adding the two numerals gives nine. The number in the 10s place is one less than the number you are multiplying by nine.

With each answer, the numeral in the 10s place increases and the numeral in the 1s place decreases.

So if you are stuck trying to think of 6 x 9, remember that it is in the 50s because 5 is one less than 6. Since 5 + 4 = 9, the answer is 54.

MULTIPLICATION FACTS

0 x 1 = 0	0 x 2 = 0	0 x 3 = 0	0 x 4 = 0
1 x 1 = 1	1 x 2 = 2	1 x 3 = 3	1 x 4 = 4
2 x 1 = 2	2 x 2 = 4	2 x 3 = 6	2 x 4 = 8
3 x 1 = 3	3 x 2 = 6	3 x 3 = 9	3 x 4 = 12
4 x 1 = 4	4 x 2 = 8	4 x 3 = 12	4 x 4 = 16
5 x 1 = 5	5 x 2 = 10	5 x 3 = 15	5 x 4 = 20
6 x 1 = 6	6 x 2 = 12	6 x 3 = 18	6 x 4 = 24
7 x 1 = 7	7 x 2 = 14	7 x 3 = 21	7 x 4 = 28
8 x 1 = 8	8 x 2 = 16	8 x 3 = 24	8 x 4 = 32
9 x 1 = 9	9 x 2 = 18	9 x 3 = 27	9 x 4 = 36
10 x 1 = 10	10 x 2 = 20	10 x 3 = 30	10 x 4 = 40

0 x 5 = 0	0 x 6 = 0	0 x 7 = 0	
1 x 5 = 5	1 x 6 = 6	1 x 7 = 7	
2 x 5 = 10	2 x 6 = 12	2 x 7 = 14	
3 x 5 = 15	3 x 6 = 18	3 x 7 = 21	
4 x 5 = 20	4 x 6 = 24	4 x 7 = 28	
5 x 5 = 25	5 x 6 = 30	5 x 7 = 35	
6 x 5 = 30	6 x 6 = 36	6 x 7 = 42	
7 x 5 = 35	7 x 6 = 42	7 x 7 = 49	
8 x 5 = 40	8 x 6 = 48	8 x 7 = 56	
9 x 5 = 45	9 x 6 = 54	9 x 7 = 63	
10 x 5 = 50	10 x 6 = 60	10 x 7 = 70	

0 x 8 = 0	0 x 9 = 0	0 x 10 = 0	
1 x 8 = 8	1 x 9 = 9	1 x 10 = 10	
2 x 8 = 16	2 x 9 = 18	2 x 10 = 20	
3 x 8 = 24	3 x 9 = 27	3 x 10 = 30	
4 x 8 = 32	4 x 9 = 36	4 x 10 = 40	
5 x 8 = 40	5 x 9 = 45	5 x 10 = 50	
6 x 8 = 48	6 x 9 = 54	6 x 10 = 60	
7 x 8 = 56	7 x 9 = 63	7 x 10 = 70	
8 x 8 = 64	8 x 9 = 72	8 x 10 = 80	
9 x 8 = 72	9 x 9 = 81	9 x 10 = 90	
10 x 8 = 80	10 x 9 = 90	10 x 10 = 100	

Name _____

 MULTIPLICATION ASSESSMENT

1. **12** x **2** = ___   2. **11** x **6** = ___   3. **0** x **1** = ___

4. **3** x **1** = ___   5. **12** x **3** = ___   6. **2** x **2** = ___

7. **11** x **3** = ___   8. **0** x **0** = ___   9. **7** x **5** = ___

10. **6** x **9** = ___   11. **5** x **6** = ___   12. **10** x **4** = ___

13. **8** x **7** = ___   14. **7** x **7** = ___   15. **1** x **2** = ___

16. **2** x **5** = ___   17. **3** x **4** = ___   18. **4** x **0** = ___

19. **0** x **2** = ___   20. **1** x **6** = ___   21. **9** x **4** = ___

22. **10** x **6** = ___   23. **5** x **3** = ___   24. **10** x **7** = ___

25. **8** x **8** = ___   26. **7** x **4** = ___   27. **5** x **8** = ___

28. **4** x **6** = ___   29. **12** x **6** = ___   30. **1** x **1** = ___

31. **9** x **9** = ___   32. **10** x **11** = ___   33. **2** x **6** = ___

34. **4** x **2** = ___   35. **3** x **3** = ___   36. **11** x **8** = ___

37. **7** x **9** = ___   38. **3** x **0** = ___   39. **11** x **11** = ___

40. **9** x **8** = ___   41. **9** x **5** = ___   42. **2** x **3** = ___

43. **10** x **10** = ___   44. **4** x **8** = ___   45. **10** x **5** = ___

MULTIPLICATION ASSESSMENT

46. **11 x 6 =** ___   47. **8 x 2 =** ___   48. **3 x 8 =** ___

49. **0 x 5 =** ___   50. **11 x 2 =** ___   51. **12 x 0 =** ___

52. **6 x 3 =** ___   53. **0 x 8 =** ___   54. **11 x 2 =** ___

55. **11 x 9 =** ___   56. **10 x 3 =** ___   57. **4 x 4 =** ___

58. **1 x 4 =** ___   59. **9 x 1 =** ___   60. **11 x 1 =** ___

61. **11 x 5 =** ___   62. **2 x 9 =** ___   63. **5 x 1 =** ___

64. **12 x 8 =** ___   65. **6 x 8 =** ___   66. **11 x 0 =** ___

67. **10 x 1 =** ___   68. **10 x 8 =** ___   69. **9 x 3 =** ___

70. **10 x 9 =** ___   71. **10 x 12 =** ___   72. **5 x 5 =** ___

73. **2 x 7 =** ___   74. **1 x 8 =** ___   75. **12 x 9 =** ___

76. **12 x 12 =** ___   77. **9 x 0 =** ___   78. **6 x 6 =** ___

79. **3 x 7 =** ___   80. **10 x 2 =** ___   81. **10 x 10 =** ___

82. **12 x 7 =** ___   83. **11 x 4 =** ___   84. **12 x 1 =** ___

85. **1 x 7 =** ___   86. **7 x 6 =** ___   87. **12 x 4 =** ___

88. **12 x 5 =** ___   89. **5 x 4 =** ___   90. **7 x 0 =** ___

TLC10200 Copyright © Teaching & Learning Company, Carthage, IL 62321-0010

LESSON PLAN 7
DIVISION

INTRODUCTION: Recall division of whole numbers. $12 \div 4 = ?$ asks how many groups of four can be found in a group of 12. The answer is three.

In division of fractions, ($1/2 \div 1/4 = ?$) we are asking how many $1/4$s can be found in $1/2$. For division of fractions, we invert the divisor (flip over the second fraction) and multiply.

$$1/2 \div 1/4 = 1/2 \times 4/1 = 4/2 = 2$$

(For a complete discussion of division of fractions, see the *Math Phonics™–Fractions* book.)

NOTE TO PARENTS: Send home note 4 on page 59.

HOMEWORK: Worksheets Q, R and S (pages 66-68).

DIVISION ASSESSMENT: After students have studied the division facts and rules of divisibility, give the assessment.

MATH HISTORY BONUS: It took nearly two centuries for the decimal system popularized in Baghdad to reach Spain. There it was called Ghobar numerals from the Arabic word for *sand* as sandboxes were occasionally used instead of paper to compute a problem.

DIVISION OF DECIMALS: Look at this decimal problem:

$$5 \overline{)2.5}$$

The answer will have a 5 in it, but where is the decimal? Is the answer 5 or .05 or .5? Look at it as a fraction.

$$2\,5/10 \div 5 = 25/10 \times 1/5 = 25/50 = 1/2$$

The decimal answer must be the same, so .5 is the answer.

$$5 \overline{)2.5}^{\,.5}$$

To get the correct answer, put the decimal directly above the decimal in the bracket. Then divide.

Give the class some other examples to try.

$$6\overline{)3.6}^{\,.6} \qquad 4\overline{)2.8}^{\,.7} \qquad 9\overline{).63}^{\,.07} \qquad 2\overline{).08}^{\,.04}$$

What about $.5\overline{)25}$?

It seems that .5 ($1/2$) should fit into 25 fifty times. Do this as a fraction.

$$25/1 \div 5/10 = 25/1 \times 10/5 = 250/5 = 50$$

The answer is 50. To get that answer without using fractions, make the original problem $5\overline{)250}$ just as in the third step of the fraction problem. Do this by moving the decimal to the right of the divisor to make it a whole number. Then move the decimal in the bracket the same number of places. Then divide.

$$.5\overline{)25.0}^{\,5\,0.}$$

Try some other examples:

$$.4\overline{)1.2} \qquad .2\overline{)6.0} \qquad .3\overline{)1.2}$$

DIVIDING DECIMALS

Directions: Put the decimal point in the correct place in each problem.

1. 5)2.5 with 0 5 above
2. 5).25 with 0 5 above
3. 3)1.2 with 0 4 above
4. 3).12 with 0 4 above
5. 6)2.4 with 0 4 above

6. 6)4.8 with 0 8 above
7. 7).63 with 0 9 above
8. 6)4.2 with 0 7 above
9. 6)5.4 with 0 9 above
10. 6).54 with 0 9 above

Directions: Divide. Put the decimal point in the correct place.

11. 7)4.9
12. 7).49
13. 8).56
14. 7).63

Directions: Multiply. Count decimal places.

15. 13
    x .4

16. 25
    x .6

17. 1.3
    x .4

18. 3.2
    x 8

19. 65
    x .4

20. 6.5
    x .4

Directions: Add. Keep decimals in a straight line.

21. 1.4 + 2.58 = _____
22. 2.93 + 7.8 = _____
23. 15.9 + 39.84 = _____

24. 16 + 23.8 = _____
25. 45.33 + 26 = _____
26. 98.8 + 13.24 = _____

27. If you rode your mountain bike 18.8 kilometers in 2 hours, how far did you go in one hour? _____

28. If 3 safety pins are laid end to end and measure .12 meters, how long is one safety pin? _____

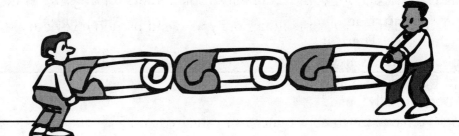

CHALLENGE:
If three pairs of jogging shoes cost $119.85, how much would five pairs cost? _____

Name _____

WORKSHEET R

DIVIDING DECIMALS

Directions: Divide. Keep the decimal point in the answer directly above the decimal point inside the bracket.

1. $3\overline{)\,.6}$ 2. $4\overline{)\,.08}$ 3. $5\overline{)\,2.5}$ 4. $6\overline{)\,3.6}$ 5. $6\overline{)\,.36}$

6. $7\overline{)\,4.9}$ 7. $8\overline{)\,5.6}$ 8. $9\overline{)\,2.7}$ 9. $8\overline{)\,.32}$ 10. $6\overline{)\,.42}$

Directions: Divide. Move the decimal in the divisor to make it a whole number. (.5˄) Move the decimal inside the bracket the same number of places. (3.5˄)

Example: $.5_˄\overline{)\,3.5_˄}$

11. $.2\overline{)\,1.2}$ 12. $.5\overline{)\,1.5}$ 13. $.6\overline{)\,.18}$ 14. $.03\overline{)\,.27}$ 15. $.7\overline{)\,4.9}$

16. $.9\overline{)\,8.1}$ 17. $.04\overline{)\,.016}$ 18. $.8\overline{)\,.24}$ 19. $.5\overline{)\,4.5}$ 20. $.8\overline{)\,.72}$

21. You have an 8.5-meter piece of wood trim for a craft project. It needs to be cut into pieces .5 meters long. How many pieces will you be able to cut? _____

22. If a beef roast weighs 1.8 kilograms and will be used to serve 9 people, how many kilograms will each person get? _____

23. On the first day of school, your homework took 2 hours for English, 1.5 hours for science and .25 hours for math. How many hours did you spend on homework in all? _____

CHALLENGE:

It's Halloween! You have bought 8.5 ounces of candy corn, 10.25 ounces of candy bars and 4.2 ounces of hard candy. If 9 trick-or-treaters come and each one gets the same number of ounces, how many ounces will each one get? _____

TLC10200 Copyright © Teaching & Learning Company, Carthage, IL 62321-0010

LEVEL 1   **67**

DIVIDING DECIMALS

Directions: Divide.

1. $8\overline{)75.2}$ 2. $4\overline{)3.04}$ 3. $12\overline{)25.2}$ 4. $25\overline{).325}$

Directions: Divide. Move the decimal point in the divisor and inside the bracket.

5. $1.4\overline{)1.82}$ 6. $1.7\overline{).374}$ 7. $.23\overline{)25.30}$ 8. $.18\overline{).306}$

Directions: Review. Count decimal places.

9. $\begin{array}{r} 1.8 \\ \times\ 3.2 \\ \hline \end{array}$ 10. $\begin{array}{r} .16 \\ \times\ 15 \\ \hline \end{array}$ 11. $\begin{array}{r} .38 \\ \times\ 21 \\ \hline \end{array}$ 12. $\begin{array}{r} 5.9 \\ \times\ 3.8 \\ \hline \end{array}$

Directions: Review. Keep decimal points in a straight line.

13. 23.8 + 13.62 + 25 = _____   14. 95.2 + 3.86 + 21.8 = _____

15. Tacos are selling for $.75 (tax included). If the concession stand has taken in $82.50 for tacos, how many tacos were sold? _____

CHALLENGE:

If you bought $8.05 worth of gas and drove 23 miles, how much did the gas cost for one mile? _____

At the same price, how much would the gas cost if you drove 95 miles? _____

RULES OF DIVISIBILITY

2s: Any number ending in 0, 2, 4, 6 or 8 is divisible by two.

3s: Add the numerals in a number. If they add up to 3, 6 or 9, the number is divisible by 3. (Example: 21: 2 + 1 = 3 and 21 is divisible by 3. 18: 1 + 8 = 9 and 18 is divisible by 3.)

4s: Every other even number is divisible by four. Memorize this pattern:

| 4 | 8 | 12 | 16 | 20 |
| 24 | 28 | 32 | 36 | 40 |

5s: Numbers ending in 0 or 5 are divisible by 5.

6s: Add the numerals in a number. If they add up to 3, 6 or 9 and the number is an even number, it is divisible by 6. (Example: 24: 2 + 4 = 6 and 24 is even–24 is divisible by 6.)

7s: Memorize the numbers divisible by seven.

8s: Numbers divisible by eight are always even. Memorize this pattern:

| 8 | 16 | 24 | 32 | 40 |
| 48 | 56 | 64 | 72 | 80 |

9s: Add the numerals in a number. If they add up to nine, the number is divisible by nine.

10s: Numbers ending in zero are divisible by 10.

Give the class some numbers and have them use these rules to find all the divisors of the numbers.

DIVISION ASSESSMENT

1. **50 ÷ 5 = ____**   2. **2 ÷ 2 = ____**   3. **16 ÷ 8 = ____**

4. **4 ÷ 4 = ____**   5. **18 ÷ 9 = ____**   6. **5)‾2‾5‾**

7. **4)‾1‾2‾**   8. **9 ÷ 9 = ____**   9. **1 ÷ 1 = ____**

10. **4 ÷ 2 = ____**   11. **5)‾2‾0‾**   12. **9)‾2‾7‾**

13. **2)‾6‾**   14. **4)‾3‾6‾**   15. **4)‾0‾**

16. **4)‾1‾6‾**   17. **8)‾4‾8‾**   18. **8)‾8‾**

19. **9)‾3‾6‾**   20. **4)‾8‾**   21. **5)‾1‾5‾**

22. **8)‾2‾4‾**   23. **9)‾4‾5‾**   24. **5)‾0‾**

25. **8)‾3‾2‾**   26. **5)‾4‾5‾**   27. **9)‾5‾4‾**

28. **2)‾8‾**   29. **9)‾6‾3‾**   30. **2)‾1‾0‾**

31. **9)‾7‾2‾**   32. **4)‾2‾8‾**   33. **4)‾2‾0‾**

34. **9)‾8‾1‾**   35. **2)‾1‾6‾**   36. **2)‾1‾2‾**

37. **9)‾0‾**   38. **4)‾3‾2‾**   39. **2)‾1‾4‾**

DIVISION ASSESSMENT

40. $2\overline{)18}$ 41. $8\overline{)56}$ 42. $5\overline{)40}$

43. $4\overline{)24}$ 44. $8\overline{)0}$ 45. $2\overline{)0}$

46. $5\overline{)30}$ 47. $5\overline{)35}$ 48. $8\overline{)64}$

49. $8\overline{)80}$ 50. $8\overline{)72}$ 51. $3\overline{)6}$

52. $1\overline{)0}$ 53. $3\overline{)12}$ 54. $10\overline{)70}$

55. $3\overline{)3}$ 56. $6\overline{)6}$ 57. $1\overline{)9}$

58. $3\overline{)9}$ 59. $5\overline{)5}$ 60. $10\overline{)20}$

61. $7\overline{)56}$ 62. $3\overline{)15}$ 63. $1\overline{)2}$

64. $10\overline{)10}$ 65. $7\overline{)7}$ 66. $10\overline{)0}$

67. $3\overline{)18}$ 68. $10\overline{)80}$ 69. $1\overline{)3}$

70. $10\overline{)30}$ 71. $7\overline{)49}$ 72. $1\overline{)8}$

73. $7\overline{)63}$ 74. $3\overline{)21}$ 75. $3\overline{)27}$

76. $7\overline{)42}$ 77. $10\overline{)40}$ 78. $7\overline{)0}$

DIVISION ASSESSMENT

79. $1 \overline{)4}$　　　　80. $3 \overline{)24}$　　　　81. $7 \overline{)35}$

82. $10 \overline{)90}$　　　83. $1 \overline{)6}$　　　　84. $10 \overline{)60}$

85. $1 \overline{)5}$　　　　86. $10 \overline{)100}$　　87. $1 \overline{)7}$

88. $6 \overline{)0}$　　　　89. $6 \overline{)36}$　　　　90. $3 \overline{)0}$

91. $7 \overline{)28}$　　　92. $6 \overline{)54}$　　　93. $6 \overline{)42}$

94. $6 \overline{)12}$　　　95. $6 \overline{)24}$　　　96. $7 \overline{)21}$

97. $6 \overline{)48}$　　　98. $6 \overline{)18}$　　　99. $7 \overline{)14}$

100. $6 \overline{)60}$　　101. $4 \overline{)40}$　　102. $5 \overline{)10}$

103. $9 \overline{)90}$　　104. $8 \overline{)40}$　　105. $2 \overline{)20}$

106. $3 \overline{)30}$　　107. $1 \overline{)10}$　　108. $6 \overline{)30}$

109. $7 \overline{)70}$　　110. $10 \overline{)50}$

INTRODUCTION: Sometimes a fraction is called a *ratio*.

If a family has four kids and one is a girl, we could say the *ratio* of girls to children in the family is 1 to 4 or $1/4$.

Another family might have eight children, two of which are girls, and we could say the *ratio* of girls to children in the family is 2 to 8 or $2/8$.

1 to 4 or $1/4$ 2 to 8 or $2/8$

Since $2/8$ can be reduced to $1/4$, we can say the *ratio* of girls to children in both families is the same—$1/4$.

Have students name other fractions equivalent to $1/4$ and $2/8$.

$3/12$ $5/20$ $25/100$ and others

PERCENT: When a ratio refers to a group of 100, we can use the term *percent*. If a school had 100 students and 25 of the students were girls, we could say the ratio of girls to students is 25 to 100 or $25/100$ or .25 or 25%.

If another class had 20 students and 5 were girls, we could say the ratio of girls to students is 5 to 20 or $5/20$.

In all of these examples, $1/4$ of the people are girls. It is sometimes easier to think of ratios as percents. You know that if you are talking about 25% of a group you mean $1/4$ of the group.

Ask the class if they remember how to change to an equivalent fraction.

$$\frac{1 \times 25}{4 \times 25} = \frac{25}{100}$$

Multiply the numerator and denominator by the same number.

100% CIRCLE: There are many ways to picture percent. Give each student a copy of the 100% circle (page 75), a vinyl page protector and a crayon.

Ask students to count 25 of the small segments and color them to picture 25% of the circle. (Remind them that a 25¢ piece is sometimes called a quarter because it is $1/4$ of a dollar.)

Can they tell you how many of the segments would have to be colored to picture half of the circle? Have them color 50 to see that this is correct. One half of a group can be called 50% of the group. (A 50-cent piece is also called a half dollar.)

Most people do not color circles to find percents. Here is an easier way.

Example: If $1/5$ of the class is sick, what percent would that be? We would know the percent if we know this equivalent fraction: $1/5 = ?/100$

Five times 20 equals 100 so

$$\frac{1 \times 20}{5 \times 20} = \frac{20}{100}$$

If we know we have the ratio 20 per 100, we know we have 20%.

What about .20? How would you write that as a fraction?

$$.20 = {}^{20}/_{100}$$

What percent would .20 be?

$$.20 = {}^{20}/_{100} = 20\%$$

HOMEWORK: Worksheets T, U and V (pages 77-79).

MATH HISTORY BONUS: By the late 13th century, the city-state of Florence, Italy, was passing laws against the dangerous "decimals." This was to protect honest citizens against bank forgers who could easily change amounts by tampering with a 0, 6 or 9.

HOW TO FIGURE TIPS IN RESTAURANTS: This can be used as extra credit, or you can teach this to the entire class. It is rather easy to teach and gives students a feeling of power over numbers.

100% CIRCLE

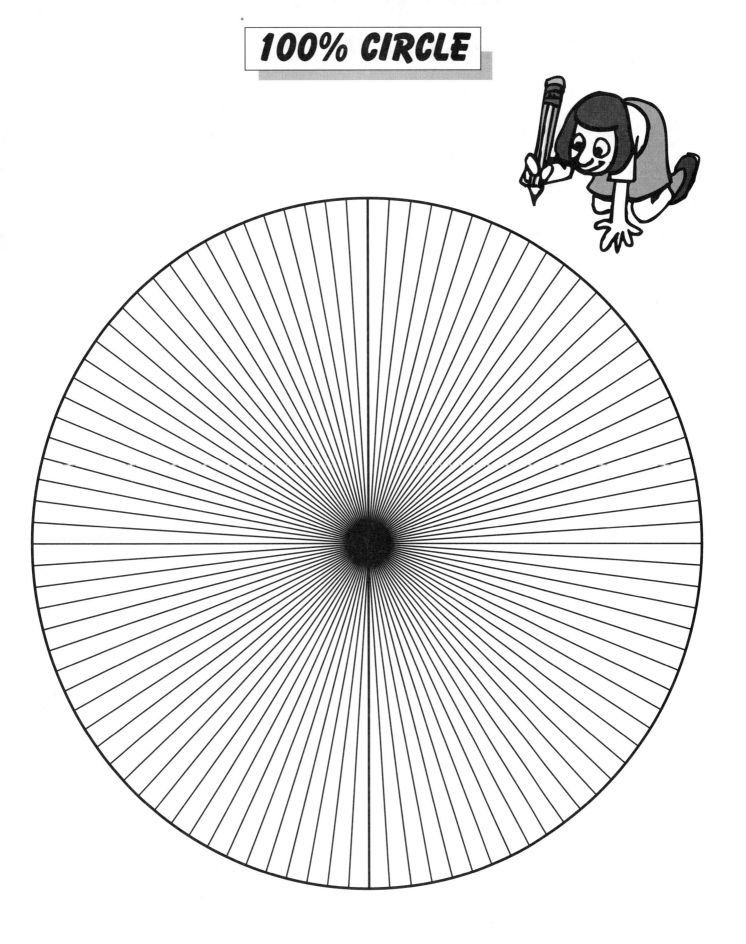

FIGURING TIPS

When you are paying your bill in a restaurant, it is considered good manners to add a tip for the waiter or waitress. Most people pay 15% of their total bill. If we know 10% of the bill and 5% of the bill, we can add them to get 15% of the bill.

This can be done as mental math by following these rules:

1. Round off the bill to the nearest dollar to make it easier to figure. (Ex: The bill is $9.87 and you round it off to $10.00 for easier mental math. For 50¢, round to the larger dollar.)

2. Find 10% of the bill ($^1/_{10}$ of the bill) by moving the decimal point one place to the left. If you can't remember which way to move the decimal, try moving it both ways. $^1/_{10}$ will give you a smaller amount.

   $10.00—one place to the left is $1.00

   $10.00—one place to the right is $100.00

3. Now think of half of the 10% to get 5% of the bill.

   Half of $1.00 is 50¢.

4. Add the 10% amount and the 5% amount to get the tip.

   $1.00 + $.50 = $1.50

Try these sample problems:

A. Your bill is $19.60.

   Round off to $20.00
   10% is $2.00
   5% is $1.00
   Tip is $3.00

B. Your bill is $8.70.

   Round off to $9.00
   10% is $.90
   5% is $.45
   Tip is $1.35

Teach this to a relative or friend. Have them sign below.

I have learned to figure tips as mental math.

Signed _____

RATIOS AND PERCENTS

Directions: Use equivalent fractions to complete each ratio.

1. $\dfrac{1}{4} \times \dfrac{3}{3} = \dfrac{3}{12}$

2. $\dfrac{1}{5} = \dfrac{}{10}$

3. $\dfrac{1}{2} = \dfrac{}{20}$

4. $\dfrac{1}{3} = \dfrac{}{12}$

5. $\dfrac{10}{20} = \dfrac{}{100}$

6. $\dfrac{1}{4} = \dfrac{}{100}$

7. $\dfrac{2}{5} = \dfrac{}{100}$

8. $\dfrac{7}{10} = \dfrac{}{100}$

Directions: Write each fraction as a percent.

9. $\dfrac{25}{100} = 25\%$

10. $\dfrac{5}{100} = \underline{\quad}\%$

11. $\dfrac{75}{100} = \underline{\quad}\%$

12. $\dfrac{28}{100} = \underline{\quad}\%$

13. $\dfrac{45}{100} = \underline{\quad}\%$

14. $\dfrac{3}{100} = \underline{\quad}\%$

15. $\dfrac{66}{100} = \underline{\quad}\%$

16. $\dfrac{95}{100} = \underline{\quad}\%$

Directions: Write each decimal as a percent.

17. .50 = 50%

18. .25 = _____%

19. .03 = _____%

20. .75 = _____%

21. .60 = _____%

22. .05 = _____%

Directions: Change to an equivalent fraction then to a percent.

23. $\dfrac{1}{20} = \dfrac{}{100} = \underline{\quad}\%$

24. $\dfrac{1}{5} = \dfrac{}{100} = \underline{\quad}\%$

25. $\dfrac{9}{10} = \dfrac{}{100} = \underline{\quad}\%$

26. Twelve of the 20 students in your class got As on their report cards. What percent is that?

_____

27. Four out of five people surveyed said their favorite day of the week was Friday. What fraction is that? What percent? _____

CHALLENGE:

Football tickets are on sale at 3 for $39.00. What would be the price of 8 tickets? _____

RATIOS AND PERCENTS

Directions: Change each to a fraction and then to a percent.

1.
$$.03 = \frac{\quad}{100} = \underline{\quad}\%$$

2.
$$.30 = \frac{\quad}{100} = \underline{\quad}\%$$

3.
$$.99 = \frac{\quad}{100} = \underline{\quad}\%$$

Directions: What is the tip for each of these restaurant bills?

4. $10.00
    10% = $1.00
    5% = $.50
    15% = $1.50

5. $20.00
    10% = _____
    5% = _____
    15% = _____

6. $8.00
    10% = _____
    5% = _____
    15% = _____

7. Your family ate out. The bill was $4.25 for burgers, $2.50 for fries, $3.00 for salads and $2.15 for drinks. How much is the total bill? _____ How much is the tip? _____

Directions: Divide.

8. $.7\overline{)2.87}$
    9. $3\overline{)36.3}$
    10. $4\overline{).16}$
    11. $.5\overline{)5.25}$
    12. $.3\overline{)9.3}$

13. Six of the 25 girls in the class have blond hair. What

    percent of the girls have blond hair?_____

Color in a Bottle

CHALLENGE:

Write out these letters to form the mystery message.

    a. the first .50 of the word YOUR
    b. the first .5 of the word UP
    c. the first 50% of the word WISH
    d. the last 50% of the word ON.

    __ __ __ __ __ __
    a a   b   c c   d

RATIOS AND PERCENTS

Directions: Change each to hundredths and then to a percent.

1. $\dfrac{1}{20} = \dfrac{}{100} = $ _____%

2. $\dfrac{2}{25} = \dfrac{}{100} = $ _____%

3. $\dfrac{7}{20} = \dfrac{}{100} = $ _____%

4. $\dfrac{19}{20} = \dfrac{}{100} = $ _____%

5. $\dfrac{24}{25} = \dfrac{}{100} = $ _____%

6. $\dfrac{49}{50} = \dfrac{}{100} = $ _____%

Directions: Reduce each fraction. Then change to a percent.

7. $\dfrac{7}{28} = $

8. $\dfrac{26}{52} = $

9. $\dfrac{49}{98} = $

10. $\dfrac{27}{36} = $

11. $\dfrac{21}{28} = $

12. $\dfrac{9}{36} = $

Directions: Divide.

13. $12\overline{)21.6}$

14. $1.2\overline{)21.6}$

15. $.18\overline{)3.78}$

16. $2.6\overline{)5.46}$

17. $1.9\overline{).589}$

18. $.24\overline{).744}$

Directions: Review.

19. $\begin{array}{r} 7.6 \\ \times\ 9.8 \\ \hline \end{array}$

20. $\begin{array}{r} 3.29 \\ \times\ 56 \\ \hline \end{array}$

21. $353 - 274.98 = $ _____

CHALLENGE:

How many different numbers less than 1000 can you make using a 0, 6 and/or a 9? On the back of this paper, list all of them. (The numbers can have one, two or three numerals.) You may use a numeral more than once.

LESSON PLAN 9
FRACTIONS AND PERCENTS

INTRODUCTION: Remind students of the rule for fractions in Lesson Plan 1.

RULE: A fraction is a number that shows that something or a group of items has been divided. It has a numerator above the line and a denominator below the line.

Recall that when you have an improper fraction, you divide to find the mixed number or whole number.

$$8/4 = 4\overline{)8}\;^2 = 2$$

$$7/4 = 4\overline{)\begin{array}{l}1^3/_4\\7\\ \underline{4}\\3\end{array}}= 1^3/_4$$

A proper fraction ($1/4$) also means "divide." We can divide if we add a decimal and zeros.

$$1/4 = 4\overline{)\begin{array}{l}.25\\1.00\\ \underline{8}\\20\\ \underline{20}\end{array}} = .25 = 25/100$$

This makes sense because $25/100$ reduces to $1/4$.

FRACTIONS AND PERCENTS: In the last section, we found a percent by changing a fraction to an equivalent fraction with 100 as the denominator. Now we have another way to find a percent. Divide to find a decimal, and then change from a decimal to a percent.

$$1/5 = 5\overline{)\begin{array}{l}.20\\1.00\end{array}} = .20 = 20/100 = 20\%$$

Have students divide $1/10$ to get a decimal and a percent.

$$1/10 = 10\overline{)\begin{array}{l}.10\\1.00\end{array}} = .10 = 10/100 = 10\%$$

TLC10200 Copyright © Teaching & Learning Company, Carthage, IL 62321-0010

LESSON PLAN 9:
CONTINUED

REVIEW: Remind students that they can find 10% of a number by moving the decimal point one place to the left. This was learned in the lesson on tips in restaurants.

10% of $25.00 = $25.00 = $2.50

This will be used in Worksheets W, X and Z.

Remind students that the word *and* should only be used to denote the decimal point in a number.

534.9 is read five hundred thirty-four *and* nine tenths

Give students some other numbers to read correctly—2000.95; 2095.05; etc.

WORKSHEET Z: The curve formed by this worksheet's problems is similar to a hyperbolic curve which students will probably study in Algebra II.

HISTORY BONUS: Al-Kaski, the 15th century director of the astronomical observatory at Samarkand was one of the first to realize that fractions could be written as decimals and computation would be easier.

FRACTIONS AND PERCENTS

Directions: Change each to a decimal by dividing. Show work.

1. $\dfrac{1}{4}$ = $4\overline{)\begin{array}{r}.25\\1.00\\8\\\overline{20}\end{array}}$

2. $\dfrac{1}{5}$ =

3. $\dfrac{7}{20}$ =

4. $\dfrac{3}{10}$ =

5. $\dfrac{3}{4}$ =

6. $\dfrac{4}{5}$ =

Directions: Change each to a decimal, fraction and percent. Show work.

7. $\dfrac{2}{4}$ = $4\overline{)\begin{array}{r}.50\\2.00\\20\\\overline{00}\end{array}}$ = $\dfrac{50}{100}$ = 50%

8. $\dfrac{3}{5}$ =

9. $\dfrac{13}{20}$ =

10. $\dfrac{7}{10}$ =

Directions: In figuring tips, we can find 10% of a number by moving the decimal point one place to the left.

11. 10% of 30.0 = _____   12. 10% of 65.0 = _____   13. 10% of 86.0 = _____

Directions: Find 10%. Then find 20% by multiplying by 2.

14. 10% of 23.0 = _____   15. 10% of 600 = _____   16. 10% of 325 = _____

17. 20% of 23.0 = _____   18. 20% of 600 = _____   19. 20% of 325 = _____

20. A dress sells for $75.00. It is on sale at 30% off. What is 30% of $75.00? _____

What is the sale price? _____

CHALLENGE:

Your body is about 70% water. If you weigh 350 kilograms, how many kilograms would be water? _____

FRACTIONS AND PERCENTS

Directions: Complete the chart.

1.	10%	20%	40%	40% off
$25.00	$2.50	$5.00	$10.00	$15.00
$75.00				
$120.00				

Directions: Change each to a decimal by dividing.

2. $\dfrac{1}{2} = 2\overline{)\begin{array}{c}.50\\1.00\\\underline{1\ 0}\\0\end{array}}$

3. $\dfrac{1}{4} =$

4. $\dfrac{1}{10} =$

5. $\dfrac{11}{20} =$

6. $\dfrac{19}{20} =$

7. $\dfrac{3}{4} =$

Directions: Divide to hundredths. Write the remainder as a fraction. Reduce the fraction.

8. $\dfrac{1}{8} = 8\overline{)\begin{array}{c}.12^{4/8}\\1.00\\\underline{8}\\20\\\underline{16}\\4\end{array}} = .12^{1/2}$

9. $\dfrac{7}{8} =$

10. $\dfrac{1}{3} =$

11. $\dfrac{5}{6} =$

Directions: Write each number in decimal form.

12. _____   five hundred and twenty-three hundredths.
13. _____   five hundred twenty and three hundredths.
14. _____   five hundred twenty-three and three hundredths.
15. _____   five and twenty-three hundredths.

CHALLENGE:

Seven out of 11 of the people surveyed liked the Burger Barn's new Barbeque Bacon Burger. Write that as a ratio, change to a decimal and then to a percent. _____

FRACTIONS AND DECIMALS

Change each fraction to hundredths by dividing on another piece of paper. (Make your work easy! Equivalent fractions are equal to the same decimal–$^1/_2$ = .50 and $^2/_4$ = 5.0) Write remainders as fractions.

$\frac{1}{2}$ = _____ $\frac{2}{2}$ = _____

$\frac{1}{3}$ = _____ $\frac{2}{3}$ = _____ $\frac{3}{3}$ = _____

$\frac{1}{4}$ = _____ $\frac{2}{4}$ = _____ $\frac{3}{4}$ = _____ $\frac{4}{4}$ = _____

$\frac{1}{5}$ = _____ $\frac{2}{5}$ = _____ $\frac{3}{5}$ = _____ $\frac{4}{5}$ = _____ $\frac{5}{5}$ = _____

$\frac{1}{6}$ = _____ $\frac{2}{6}$ = _____ $\frac{3}{6}$ = _____ $\frac{4}{6}$ = _____ $\frac{5}{6}$ = _____ $\frac{6}{6}$ = _____

$\frac{1}{8}$ = ___ $\frac{2}{8}$ = ___ $\frac{3}{8}$ = ___ $\frac{4}{8}$ = ___ $\frac{5}{8}$ = ___ $\frac{6}{8}$ = ___ $\frac{7}{8}$ = ___ $\frac{8}{8}$ = ___

$\frac{1}{10}$ = __ $\frac{2}{10}$ = __ $\frac{3}{10}$ = __ $\frac{4}{10}$ = __ $\frac{5}{10}$ = __ $\frac{6}{10}$ = __ $\frac{7}{10}$ = __ $\frac{8}{10}$ = __ $\frac{9}{10}$ = __ $\frac{10}{10}$ = __

CHALLENGE:

You need to find the decimal value of 49/56. Make your work easy. Find an equivalent fraction above. What is the decimal value? _____

Name _____

PERCENTS

Mental math! Fill in the blanks. Then draw a line between each pair of dots that have the same answer. The first one has been done for you.

● 10% of 200 = __20__

— 10% of 300 = _____

— 20% of 500 = _____

— 50% of 100 = _____

— 10% of 750 = _____

— 40% of 100 = _____

— 10% of 100 = _____

— 80% of 100 = _____

— 20% of 300 = _____

— 25% of 100 = _____

— 5% of 100 = _____

10% of 50 =

50% of 50 =

60% of 100 =

40% of 200 =

20% of 50 =

20% of 200 =

75% of 100 =

10% of 500 =

50% of 200 =

20% of 150 =

20% of 100 = 20

RULES AND ASSESSMENTS: Give each student a copy of the rules on page 87 and go over them. This is a review of what has been covered in this book. Do several examples for each rule. Have students do the examples on scratch paper.

Use bingo and flash cards to give students practice with decimals.

Divide students into pairs to practice with flash cards for adding, subtracting and multiplying decimals.

Give each pair of students a set of bingo calling cards. Let students drill each other.

Have students review the graded worksheets that they have saved in their math folders.

After the class has reviewed each part of decimals, give the Assessment, Level 1 or Assessment, Level 2 (pages 88 and 89).

RULES FOR WORKING WITH DECIMALS

FRACTION: A number having a numerator (above the line) and a denominator (below the line). It shows that one object or several objects have been divided.

DECIMAL: Short way of writing a fraction that has 10 or 100 as the denominator. $5/10 = .5$ $53/100 = .53$ $3/100 = .03$

READING DECIMALS: When reading a number with a decimal point, say the word *and* for the decimal point and not at any other part of the number.

ADDITION AND SUBTRACTION: Keep decimals in a straight line.

KEY WORDS: Look for key words in word problems. Usually the last key word in a problem tells you whether to add, subtract, multiply or divide.

MULTIPLYING DECIMALS: Count the decimal places in the problem. Put the same number of decimal places in the answer.

$$
\begin{array}{rl}
.3 & = 1 \text{ decimal place} \\
\underline{\times .5} & = 1 \text{ decimal place} \\
.15 & = 2 \text{ decimal places}
\end{array}
$$

DIVIDING DECIMALS: When dividing a whole number into a decimal, put the decimal in the answer directly above the decimal inside the bracket.

$$4\overline{)3.6}\;\;\;.9 \qquad\qquad 4\overline{)3\!\uparrow\!6}\;\;\;9$$

When dividing a decimal by a decimal, move the decimal point to the right of the divisor. Move the decimal inside the bracket the same number of places.

$$.6\,\overline{).24} \qquad\qquad .6\,\overline{).24}\;\;\;.4$$

RATIO: A ratio between two numbers can be written as a fraction.

Three out of four people have brown hair = $3/4$ have brown hair.

PERCENT: When a ratio refers to a group of 100, we call it a percent.

75 out of 100 have brown hair = $75/100$ = 75% have brown hair.

FRACTIONS TO PERCENTS: A fraction can be changed to a percent by dividing the numerator by the denominator, writing as a fraction and then as a percent.

$$
1/4 = 4\overline{)1.00}\;\;\;.25 = 25/100 = 25\% \\
\phantom{1/4 = 4\overline{)1.00}}\underline{8} \\
\phantom{1/4 = 4\overline{)1.00}}\underline{20} \\
\phantom{1/4 = 4\overline{)1.00}}\underline{20}
$$

GAMES: Decimal Bingo

Decimal Flash Cards

Name _____

ASSESSMENT

Directions: Use this number: 368.59

1. Number in the tenths place _____

2. Number in the tens place _____

3. Number in the ones place _____

4. Number in the hundreds place _____

Directions: Write the decimal for each.

5. $3\frac{9}{10}$ = _____   6. $\frac{5}{100}$ = _____   7. $\frac{50}{100}$ = _____   8. $4\frac{23}{100}$ = _____   9. $23\frac{3}{100}$ = _____

10. How many pennies in a dollar? _____   11. How many nickels in a dollar? _____

Directions: Add or subtract.

12. $\begin{array}{r} 7.6 \\ + 8.1 \\ \hline \end{array}$ 13. $\begin{array}{r} 3.1 \\ - .9 \\ \hline \end{array}$ 14. $\begin{array}{r} 9.08 \\ + 6.17 \\ \hline \end{array}$ 15. 23.8 + 5.61 = _____   16. 33.8 - 2.25 = _____

Directions: Multiply.

17. $\begin{array}{r} 1.5 \\ \times 5 \\ \hline \end{array}$ 18. $\begin{array}{r} 5.8 \\ \times .2 \\ \hline \end{array}$ 19. $\begin{array}{r} .03 \\ \times 8 \\ \hline \end{array}$ 20. $\begin{array}{r} 1.38 \\ \times 4 \\ \hline \end{array}$ 21. $\begin{array}{r} 26.6 \\ \times .5 \\ \hline \end{array}$

Directions: Divide.

22. $6\overline{)3.6}$ 23. $25\overline{).25}$ 24. $18\overline{)3.6}$ 25. $1.5\overline{)3.15}$

Directions: Write each as a ratio.

26. Three out of four people in the city own

cars. _____

27. 75 out of 100 people ate fast food during the

week. _____

Directions: Change each to an equivalent fraction.

28. $\frac{1}{3} \times \frac{4}{4} = \frac{}{12}$ 29. $\frac{1}{5} = \frac{}{100}$ 30. $\frac{1}{4} = \frac{}{100}$ 31. $\frac{3}{10} = \frac{}{100}$

Directions: Change to hundredths and percent.

32. $\frac{1}{4} = \frac{}{100} = $ _____%   33. $\frac{2}{5} = \frac{}{100} = $ _____%   34. $\frac{1}{20} = \frac{}{100} = $ _____%

35. Your restaurant bill was $8.40. Round off and find the tip.

Directions: Divide into hundredths place. Leave remainder as fraction.

36. $\frac{1}{2} = 2\overline{)1.00}^{\;.50}$ 37. $\frac{4}{10} = $ 38. $\frac{7}{8} = $

Name _____

ASSESSMENT

Directions: Write the decimal for each.

1. $^5/_{100}$ _____

2. $23^5/_{10}$ _____

3. Thirteen and three hundredths _____

4. Thirty and thirteen hundredths _____

Directions: Write the word for each.

5. Four of these make a dollar. _____

6. This is one-tenth of a dollar. _____

Directions: Add or subtract.

7. 27.8 + 49.6	8. 96.2 - 47.8	9. 135.23 + 276.98	10. 336 + 42.9 = _____	11. 28 - 1.3 = _____

Directions: Multiply.

12. 2.6 x .9	13. 35.21 x 16	14. 13.2 x 5.3	15. 16.8 x .9	16. 213 x .06

Directions: Divide.

17. $5\overline{)26.5}$ 18. $1.2\overline{)3.84}$ 19. $.11\overline{)2.31}$ 20. $.06\overline{)2.46}$

Directions: Write each as a ratio and change to a percent.

21. 7 out of 10 people got a B = _____ = _____ %

22. 13 out of 20 people like fast food = _____ = _____ %

Directions: Round off each to the nearest dollar and find the 15% tip.

23. $7.49 _____

24. $18.23 _____

25. $21.55 _____

26. $35.98 _____

Directions: Change each to hundredths and write the percent.

27. $\dfrac{3}{5} = \dfrac{}{100} = $ _____ %

28. $\dfrac{7}{20} = \dfrac{}{100} = $ _____ %

29. $\dfrac{21}{50} = \dfrac{}{100} = $ _____ %

30. A dress sells for $243.00. It is on sale for 20% off. What is the sale price? _____

Directions: Complete this magic square.

31. Magic Number: _____

	.3	.65
	.5	
	.7	

ANSWER KEY

Worksheet A, page 13

1. 2/3
2. 4/10
3. 3/5
4. 8/10
5. .5; 1.2; 3.9; 2.7; 1.9; 2.4
6. 2.4; 5.9; 9.5
7. one and nine tenths; three and seven tenths

Challenge:

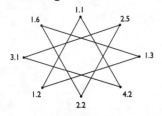

Worksheet B, page 14

1. 1 3/10
2. 2 5/10
3. .9
4. 1.4
5. 3.8
6. 8.3
7. 12.2
8. 5.5
9. 1.2; 2.1; 3.9; 8.5
10. seven and five tenths; five and seven tenths; eight and three tenths

Challenge:
 black–.1
 gray–.3
 white–.6
 not black–.9
 not white–.4
 not gray–.7

Worksheet C, page 25

1. .48
2. .73
3. .04
4. .40
5. .18

6. .07
7. 1.2
8. 10.21
9. 1.02
10. 15.25
11. five and five tenths
12. fifty and five hundredths
13. two hundred fifty and fifty hundredths
14. fifty and fifteen hundredths
15. fifteen and fifty hundredths

Challenge: 375.96

Worksheet D, page 26

2 = 2 tens = 20
3 = 3 ones = 3
4 = 4 tenths = .4
8 = 8 hundredths = .08

1. 4.5
2. 402.3
3. 8.25
4. 400.04
5. 15.5
6. 35.05
7. 154.5

Challenge: 73/100; .73

Worksheet E, page 29

1. b
2. d
3. a
4. e
5. c
6. 98.6
7. 85 pounds
8. 2.50 pounds
9. 3.5
10. 9.3 inches
11. penny = 1/100
12. dime = 10/100 = 1/10
13. nickel = 5/100 = 1/20
14. quarter = 25/100 = 1/4
15. .05

Worksheet N, page 56

1. 3.9
2. 8.4
3. .84
4. 5.52
5. .64
6. 3.24
7. .8
8. .12
9. .54
10. .56
11. 5.60 or 5.6
12. 56.00
13. 52.11
14. 59.87
15. 5.4 kilometers
16. 15.6 feet

Worksheet O, page 57

These sections should be colored:

     3.8 x .4 = 1.52
     .4 x .9 = .36
     .98 x 7 = 6.86
     .26 x 4 = 1.04
     .98 x 2 = 1.96
     5.9 x .8 = 4.72

2. 3 quarters, 1 dime, 10 pennies
3. 3.9 miles or 3.90 miles

Challenge: 384,000 kilometers

Worksheet P, page 58

	Model Stagecoach	End Table
length	5.25"	18.375"
height	4"	14"
width	3"	10.5"
door height	3.2"	11.2"
door width	.8"	2.8"
rear wheel diameter	3.5"	12.25"
front wheel diameter	2.5"	8.75"
wheel base	5.5"	19.25"
axle length	2.8"	9.8"
window width	.75"	2.625"

1. 3.04 ounces; 22.96 ounces
2. 8 pounds; 45 pounds

Challenge: 100 pounds

Worksheet Q, page 66

1. 0.5
2. .05
3. 0.4
4. .04
5. 0.4
6. 0.8
7. .09
8. 0.7
9. 0.9
10. .09
11. .7
12. .07
13. .07
14. .09
15. 5.2
16. 15.0
17. .52
18. 25.6
19. 26.0
20. 2.60
21. 3.98
22. 10.73
23. 55.74
24. 39.8
25. 71.33
26. 112.04
27. 9.4 km
28. .04 meters

Challenge: $199.75

Worksheet R, page 67

1. .2
2. .02
3. .5
4. .6
5. .06
6. .7

7. .7

8. .3

9. .04

10. .07

11. 6

12. 3

13. .3

14. 9

15. 7

16. 9

17. .4

18. .3

19. 9

20. .9

21. 17 pieces

22. .2 kilograms

23. 3.75 hours

Challenge: 2.55 ounces

Worksheet S, page 68

1. 9.4

2. .76

3. 2.1

4. .013

5. 1.3

6. .22

7. 110

8. 1.7

9. 5.76

10. 2.40

11. 7.98

12. 22.42

13. 62.42

14. 120.86

15. 110 tacos

Challenge: $.35 or 35¢; $33.25

Worksheet T, page 77

2. $\frac{1}{5} = \frac{2}{10}$

3. $\frac{1}{2} = \frac{10}{20}$

4. $\frac{1}{3} = \frac{4}{12}$

5. $\frac{10}{20} = \frac{50}{100}$

6. $\frac{1}{4} = \frac{25}{100}$

7. $\frac{2}{5} = \frac{40}{100}$

8. $\frac{7}{10} = \frac{70}{100}$

10. 5%

11. 75%

12. 28%

13. 45%

14. 3%

15. 66%

16. 95%

18. 25%

19. 3%

20. 75%

21. 60%

22. 5%

23. $\frac{5}{100} = 5\%$

24. $\frac{20}{100} = 20\%$

25. $\frac{90}{100} = 90\%$

26. 60%

27. $\frac{4}{5} = \frac{80}{100} = 80\%$

Challenge: $104.00

Worksheet U, page 78

1. $\frac{3}{100} = 3\%$

2. $\frac{30}{100} = 30\%$

3. $\frac{99}{100} = 99\%$

5. 10% = $2.00

   5% = $1.00

   15% = $3.00

6. 10% = $.80

   5% = $.40

   15% = $1.20

7. $11.90; tip is $1.80

8. 4.1

9. 12.1

10. .04

11. 10.5

12. 31

13. $\frac{6}{25} = \frac{24}{100} = 24\%$

Challenge: YOU WIN

ANSWER KEY

Worksheet V, page 79

1. $\frac{5}{100} = 5\%$
2. $\frac{8}{100} = 8\%$
3. $\frac{35}{100} = 35\%$
4. $\frac{95}{100} = 95\%$
5. $\frac{96}{100} = 96\%$
6. $\frac{98}{100} = 98\%$
7. $\frac{7}{28} = \frac{1}{4} = \frac{25}{100} = 25\%$
8. $\frac{26}{52} = \frac{1}{2} = \frac{50}{100} = 50\%$
9. $\frac{49}{98} = \frac{1}{2} = \frac{50}{100} = 50\%$
10. $\frac{27}{36} = \frac{3}{4} = \frac{75}{100} = 75\%$
11. $\frac{21}{28} = \frac{3}{4} = \frac{75}{100} = 75\%$
12. $\frac{9}{36} = \frac{1}{4} = \frac{25}{100} = 25\%$
13. 1.8
14. 18
15. 21
16. 2.1
17. .31
18. 3.1
19. 74.48
20. 184.24
21. 78.02

Challenge: 27 numbers: 0, 6, 9, 60, 66, 69, 90, 96, 99, 600, 606, 609, 660, 666, 669, 690, 696, 699, 900, 906, 909, 960, 966, 969, 990, 996, 999

Worksheet W, page 82

2. $\frac{1}{5} = .20$
3. $\frac{7}{20} = .35$
4. $\frac{3}{10} = .3$ or .30
5. $\frac{3}{4} = .75$
6. $\frac{4}{5} = .8$ or .80
8. $\frac{3}{5} = .60 = \frac{60}{100} = 60\%$
9. $\frac{13}{20} = .65 = \frac{65}{100} = 65\%$
10. $\frac{7}{10} = .70 = \frac{70}{100} = 70\%$
11. 3
12. 6.5
13. 8.6
14. 2.3
15. 60
16. 32.5

17. 4.6
18. 120
19. 65
20. $22.50; sale price $52.50

Challenge: 245 kilograms of water

Worksheet X, page 83

1.

$25.00	$2.50	$5.00	$10.00	$15.00
$75.00	$7.50	$15.00	$30.00	$45.00
$120.00	$12.00	$24.00	$48.00	$72.00

3. $\frac{1}{4} = .25$
4. $\frac{1}{10} = .1$ or .10
5. $\frac{11}{20} = .55$
6. $\frac{19}{20} = .95$
7. $\frac{3}{4} = .75$
9. $.87\frac{1}{2}$
10. $.33\frac{1}{3}$
11. $.83\frac{1}{3}$
12. 500.23
13. 520.03
14. 523.03
15. 5.23

Challenge: $\frac{7}{11} = .63\frac{7}{11} = 63\frac{7}{11}\%$

Worksheet Y, page 84

$\frac{1}{2} = $ .50		$\frac{2}{2} = $ 1.00		
$\frac{1}{3} = $ .33$\frac{1}{3}$	$\frac{2}{3} = $ .66$\frac{2}{3}$	$\frac{3}{3} = $ 1.00		
$\frac{1}{4} = $ .25	$\frac{2}{4} = $ .50	$\frac{3}{4} = $ .75	$\frac{4}{4} = $ 1.00	
$\frac{1}{5} = $ .20	$\frac{2}{5} = $ .40	$\frac{3}{5} = $ .60	$\frac{4}{5} = $ .80	$\frac{5}{5} = $ 1.00
$\frac{1}{6} = $ .16$\frac{2}{3}$	$\frac{2}{6} = $ .33$\frac{1}{3}$	$\frac{3}{6} = $ .50	$\frac{4}{6} = $ .66$\frac{2}{3}$	$\frac{5}{6} = $ .83$\frac{1}{3}$, $\frac{6}{6} = $ 1.00

$\frac{1}{8} = $ .12$\frac{1}{2}$	$\frac{2}{8} = $ .25	$\frac{3}{8} = $ .37$\frac{1}{2}$	$\frac{4}{8} = $ .50	$\frac{5}{8} = $ .62$\frac{1}{2}$	$\frac{6}{8} = $ .75	$\frac{7}{8} = $ .87$\frac{1}{2}$	$\frac{8}{8} = $ 1.00

$\frac{1}{10}$ .10	$\frac{2}{10}$ .20	$\frac{3}{10}$ .30	$\frac{4}{10}$ .40	$\frac{5}{10}$ .50	$\frac{6}{10}$ .60	$\frac{7}{10}$ .70	$\frac{8}{10}$ .80	$\frac{9}{10}$ .90	$\frac{10}{10}$ 1.00

Challenge: $.87\frac{1}{2}$

Worksheet Z, page 85

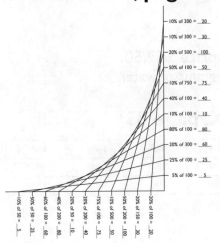

```
10% of 200 = _20_
10% of 300 = _30_
20% of 500 = _100_
50% of 100 = _50_
10% of 750 = _75_
40% of 100 = _40_
10% of 100 = _10_
80% of 100 = _80_
20% of 300 = _60_
25% of 100 = _25_
5% of 100 = _5_
```

```
10% of 50 = _5_
50% of 50 = _25_
60% of 100 = _60_
40% of 200 = _80_
20% of 50 = _10_
20% of 200 = _40_
75% of 100 = _75_
50% of 500 = _50_
20% of 200 = _100_
20% of 150 = _30_
20% of 100 = _20_
```

Assessment, Level 1, page 88

1. 5
2. 6
3. 8
4. 3
5. 3.9
6. .05
7. .50
8. 4.23
9. 23.03
10. 100
11. 20
12. 15.7
13. 2.2
14. 15.25
15. 29.41
16. 31.55
17. 7.5
18. 11.6
19. .24
20. 5.52
21. 13.30
22. .6
23. .01
24. .2
25. 2.1
26. 3/4
27. 75/100
28. 4/12

29. 20/100
30. 25/100
31. 30/100
32. 25/100 = 25%
33. 40/100 = 40%
34. 5/100 = 5%
35. $8.00; tip = $1.20
37. .40
38. .87⁴/₈ or .87¹/₂

Assessment, Level 2, page 89

1. .05
2. 23.5
3. 13.03
4. 30.13
5. quarter
6. dime
7. 77.4
8. 48.4
9. 412.21
10. 378.9
11. 26.7
12. 2.34
13. 563.36
14. 69.96
15. 15.12
16. 12.78
17. 5.3
18. 3.2
19. 21.
20. 41.
21. 7/10 = 70%
22. 13/20 = 65%
23. $7.00; $1.05 tip
24. $18.00; $2.70 tip
25. $22.00; $3.30 tip
26. $36.00; $5.40 tip
27. 60/100 = 60%
28. 35/100 = 35%
29. 42/100 = 42%
30. $194.40
31. Magic Number = 1.5

.55	.3	.65
.6	.5	.4
.35	.7	.45